The Cricket Field

CONNELTON

Holiday Village

Swimming Pool

Golf Course

Club House

Driving Range

Kim's Stables

Home Farm

Alan Turner's
EMMERDALE
Cookbook

ALAN

TURNER'S
Emmerdale
COOKBOOK

David & Charles

**YORKSHIRE
TELEVISION**

A DAVID & CHARLES BOOK

Illustrations by John Paley
Introductory text by Keith Temple
Recipes by Rosemary Moon

EMMERDALE IS A REGISTERED TRADE MARK OF
YORKSHIRE TELEVISION LIMITED.
© 1995 YORKSHIRE TELEVISION, DAVID & CHARLES

First published 1995

Keith Temple and Rosemary Moon have asserted
their right to be identified as authors of this work in
accordance with the Copyright, Designs and Patents
Act 1988.

A catalogue record for this book is available from
the British Library.

ISBN 0 7153 0381 3

Printed in England by Butler & Tanner
for David & Charles
Brunel House   Newton Abbot   Devon

CONTENTS

INTRODUCTION

The idea that I should write a cookery book was first suggested by Shirley, my late wife. I remember laughing at her at the time – it seemed a strange notion – but she pointed out that food and, more especially, the eating of it, has been an important part of my life for more years than I care to mention! She also reminded me that it was our mutual love of things gastronomic which brought us together when I stumbled upon her 'soup kitchen'. Later I would return to give her expert advice on how to spice up her soups and perk up her meals…and then she came to work for me in The Woolpack wine bar.

One morning as she watched me prepare the day's menu she mentioned the cookery book. I did nothing for a while – I was too pre-occupied with other matters – but as my life started to take shape again Shirley's idea came back to me. Over the years I've found myself really appreciating my life and my friends, and so I decided to write a book; not just a cookery book, but a celebration of Emmerdale. The village has been very good to me over the years: I came here as an outsider, with all the typical townie's arrogant preconceptions about country life. How wrong I was! I've come to love Emmerdale with a passion. I've watched it change over the years and adapt to the times; I've seen people come and go; but the basic spirit and soul of the village has remained. I found myself wanting to share my love of this special community with the world. What better way to do it than through the universal language of food?

To make the book even more special, and more personal too, I asked my friends and neighbours to contribute some of their favourite recipes. I was overwhelmed by the response. Several of the recipes included are traditional, others are more sophisticated and some are quite surprising! They all reflect the truly eclectic nature of the village of Emmerdale. Kim Tate's contributions cater for the health conscious: husband Frank has learned to his relief that healthy eating is just as enjoyable, if not more so, as 'unhealthy' eating! Kim's recipes have surprised even the staunchest of foody traditionalists (ie me!). It may come as a shock to some that Seth threw himself into the project with gusto. His favourite recipes reflect the needs of a man who spends most of his life outdoors, a man who doesn't waste his time slaving away in a kitchen. They're easy to prepare and nutritious, and take advantage of the home-grown produce readily available to him. And then there's Annie Sugden's selection. To some, Annie's culinary skills are legendary. Her cakes and pies have been winning prizes at the Hotten Show for decades. Here, Annie offers a variety of recipes which will delight and satisfy the taste buds.

The wonderful dishes presented here will give you a real taste of Emmerdale life, but I hope this book provides you with more than just recipes. I've included snippets of village gossip and tales of events long gone. I want my book to act as a kind of literary time capsule: in years to come you will be able to dip into it and be reminded of an era when Alan Turner was the landlord of The Woolpack… you'll be able to smell the delicate aromas emanating from Annie's Aga as she opens the door of her cottage on a warm summer's day, thus informing the village that she's come home from Spain once more…on a cold snowy day when icicles hang dagger-like from the window ledges of Emmerdale Farm, you'll be able to sit with Jack and Sarah in the farm kitchen, warming your cold hands after a morning's milking…share a noisy family meal with the Glovers…dine with the Tates at Home Farm.

Emmerdale has been good to me, and I can't think of anywhere else I'd rather be. After finishing my book I hope you'll agree with me.

So read on, eat and enjoy!

THE WOOLPACK

I shall never forget the first time I saw The Woolpack. It was a cold winter's night and I'd driven up for a job interview with NY Estates at Home Farm. I was a southerner, through and through – funny how things change. The winding lanes enclosed by dark stone walls held no attraction for me. I missed the safety of neon and the bustle of city traffic. This was another world, bleak and isolated. Or so I thought. I turned into Emmerdale – Beckindale as it was then – and there was the pub in front of me, solid and welcoming. The warm glow emanating from its windows enticed me in. I was hooked!

That was in the days of meat mince pies and bar snacks – sandwiches – served by Amos Brearly and Henry Wilks. They were part of the fixtures, constant and reliable. To Mr Wilks The Woolpack was a hobby to occupy his retirement years; to Amos, it was his life. I couldn't understand that then. But I'm beginning to now. We really did think that they would go on forever. The notion of a Woolpack without Mr Wilks and Mr Brearly seemed inconceivable. But nothing lasts forever. Amos sold up – to me! And now, my name hangs above the door; I'm the man licensed to sell beer and spirits. 'You don't own the pub, though,' Amos told me just before he left. 'It's on loan to you. I merely looked after it and you've to do the same. It'll be here, long after you've gone.'

The beer is the best in North Yorkshire. Seth Armstrong will deny this fervently, yet it still doesn't deter him from spending most of his ill-gotten gains at the bar. I tell a lie; I do recall a time when Seth stood up to defend my beer. Vic Windsor, newly arrived from London, claimed Yorkshire beer tasted disgusting and resembled ice cream. Seth put him straight of course. Vic now drinks my 'ice cream' with the rest of them. I don't hear him complaining!

But to be honest, food is my weakness, not beer.

So when I bought The Woolpack I decided to give my friends the chance to sample all the delights I'd been lucky enough to indulge in on my gastronomic travels. And I wanted to cook, prepare and present the food myself. So I opened The Woolpack restaurant. I think of it as a success, even though it is now closed and The Woolpack serves a more conservative fayre. People as different as the Tates and the Sugdens frequented it, sampled my French and Italian cooking and drank nice wines, and I suppose that's what cemented the reputation I have as a bon viveur! I'm proud of that venture. Always will be. One day, if fate decides I move on from The Woolpack, I hope my customers remember me as the man who thought that food, as well as travel, broadened the mind.

When Viv and Vic Windsor first arrived in the village they put a few noses out of joint in The Woolpack. Chilled by the lack of heating in the post office and horrified by the bleak wind which howls around Emmerdale, they took shelter in the bar and sat around the fireside. When basking in the warm glow and filling themselves up with my homemade chillies and warming stews they angered some of my older customers – Vic and Viv had failed to realise that there was an unspoken pecking order in operation – incomers weren't entitled to seats by the fireside, which were reserved for respected elders. Naturally, I could not condone such a monopoly, so when The Woolpack was refurbished, I changed the layout and the menu. I now offer delicious snacks and nutritious lunches with my ever-present supply of good ales. The old days of Sam Pearson and his cronies hogging the fireside are long gone. Everyone is equal (unless you are a Dingle), and everyone is entitled to warm themselves by the fire on a cold winter's day without feeling guilty.

ALAN'S EMMERD ALE FISH BATTER

SUFFICIENT FOR 4 LARGE PIECES OF COD

The secret of the delicious fish and chips that are served in the bar at The Woolpack is the batter made, of course, with Emmerd Ale. Dip the fish into the batter, then fry at 180°C/350°F for 8–10 minutes, until golden brown. To test if the fat is hot enough, drop a small cube of bread into it – it should brown in 60 seconds. If it takes a much shorter time the fat is too hot.

4oz (120g) plain flour	*8fl oz (225ml) Emmerd*
3tbsp corn or vegetable	*Ale or other beer*
oil	*1 egg white, size 2*

Sieve the flour into a large bowl and make a well in the centre. Add the oil and the beer, then beat the ingredients together into a smooth batter. Just before use, whisk the egg white until stiff then fold it carefully into the mixture – this gives a light and crispy batter.

SHEPHERD'S CHILLI

SERVES 4

Chilli con carne is almost standard pub fare these days. I make a delicious chilli using lamb, a traditional meat in Emmerdale and Mexico, and blend herbs and spices for a richly authentic seasoning.

2tbsp oil	*1 cinnamon stick, broken*
2 large onions, sliced	*14oz (400g) can*
1–2tsp chilli powder	*chopped tomatoes*
1tsp ground cumin	*15oz (440g) can red*
1lb (460g) minced lamb	*kidney beans*
1 clove garlic, crushed	*salt and freshly ground*
1tbsp freshly chopped	*black pepper*
coriander, or 1tsp	*1tbsp red wine vinegar*
dried	*1tbsp demerara sugar*
1tbsp freshly chopped	*tortilla chips and soured*
oregano, or 1tsp dried	*cream to serve*
1 bay leaf	

Cook the onions in the oil with the chilli powder and ground cumin – cook over a low heat for about 5 minutes until the onions are soft. Add the lamb and garlic and cook quickly until the meat is well browned. Add the herbs and the cinnamon stick, then the chopped tomatoes and the liquid from the kidney beans. Bring to the boil, stir well and season with salt and pepper. Simmer for 40 minutes or so – the longer the better to allow the flavour of the chilli to develop.

Stir the kidney beans into the meat and simmer for a further 10 minutes or so, then add the vinegar and sugar. Season with extra salt and pepper as required. Serve the chilli with a spoonful of soured cream and tortilla chips.

GOOD OLD STEAK & GUINNESS PIES

MAKES 4–6 INDIVIDUAL PIES

My steak pies are a straightforward celebration of simple, gutsy flavours: steak, onions and Guinness. No fancy seasonings or extra ingredients are added eg mushrooms, oysters or mustard. The homemade shortcrust pastry gives the final caring touch – no puff pastry lid baked separately and stuck on at the last moment.

3tbsp oil	*3 large onions, sliced*
2lb (900g) stewing steak,	*salt and freshly ground*
cut into 1in (2.5cm)	*black pepper*
pieces	*³/4pt (440ml) Guinness*

FOR THE PASTRY

8oz (225g) plain flour	*2oz (60g) white cooking*
pinch of salt	*fat*
2oz (60g) butter or	*water to mix*
margarine	*milk for glazing*

Preheat the oven to 180°C/350°F/Gas 4. Heat the oil in a large frying-pan and brown the meat on all sides. Use a draining spoon to transfer the meat to an ovenproof casserole dish, then fry the onions in the remaining oil until they are well browned. Season the onions with salt and pepper, then add the Guinness and bring it to the boil, scraping up any sediment from the bottom of the pan. Pour the mixture over the meat in the casserole dish, cover and cook in the preheated oven for 2 hours. Leave the meat until cold.

Preheat the oven to 200°C/400°F/Gas 6. Prepare the pastry. Sieve the flour and salt into a bowl then add the fats, cut into small pieces. Rub in until the mixture resembles fine breadcrumbs. Add sufficient water to make a firm, manageable dough, then roll the pastry out thinly on a floured surface.

Divide the meat between 4 or 6 individual pie dishes. Line the rims of the dishes with pastry trimmings, then cover the pies with pastry tops. Seal the two layers of pastry together, then make a small slit in the middle of each pie crust, to allow the steam from the steak filling to escape. Brush the pastry with a little milk, then bake the pies on a baking sheet in the preheated oven for 25–30 minutes, until the pastry is a pale golden colour. Serve with fresh vegetables.

THE WOOLPACK YORKSHIRE APPLE CHEESECAKE

SERVES 8

This cheesecake is not rich and keeps well once cut. I sometimes serve it with cream poured all over, but it doesn't really need it.

FOR THE BASE

8oz (225g) ginger nut biscuits, very finely crushed	*3oz (90g) butter, melted* *2oz (60g) caster sugar*

FOR THE FILLING

8oz (225g) curd or sieved cottage cheese	*1¹/₂oz (45g) plain flour* *3oz (90g) Wensleydale*
¹/₂tsp mixed spice	*cheese, grated or*
grated rind and juice of half a lemon	*crumbled* *¹/₄pt (150ml) soured*
1 large Bramley apple, peeled, cored and grated	*cream* *3 eggs, size 2, separated* *4oz (120g) caster sugar*

FOR THE TOPPING

2 large Bramley apples, peeled, cored and sliced	*grated rind and juice of half a lemon* *sugar to taste*

Preheat the oven to 160°C/325°F/Gas 3. Prepare the base by mixing together the butter, sugar and biscuit crumbs. Press into the base and a little way up the sides of an 8in (20cm) springform, loose-bottomed tin. Chill until needed.

Place all the filling ingredients in a large bowl in the order listed, except for the egg whites and 2oz (60g) of the caster sugar. Beat until well mixed then set aside. Whisk the egg whites until stiff, then whisk in the remaining sugar. Fold the meringue into the cheese mixture, then pour the filling into the biscuit lined tin. Bake in the preheated oven for about 90 minutes, until risen and firm to the touch. Turn the oven off, open the door and leave the cheesecake to cool in the oven for one hour. The cheesecake may sink slightly, but don't worry!

Prepare the topping. Stew the apples with the lemon juice and rind until soft, preferably in a microwave on full power so that no added water is required. Add sugar to taste and beat until smooth, then spoon the apple mixture into the centre of the cheesecake.

Chill for at least 2 hours before serving.

CARROT AND CABBAGE CRUNCH

SERVES 12

Part of the success of The Woolpack's toasted sandwiches and filled rolls is down to the coleslaw, which is freshly made each day. The secret of the dressing is to mix the mayonnaise with yogurt – a tip which is starting to get out around the village.

¹/₂ Dutch white cabbage, finely shredded	*5tbsp mayonnaise* *3tbsp natural yogurt*
3 large carrots, peeled and coarsely grated	*salt and freshly ground black pepper*
¹/₂ small onion, finely chopped	

Ensure that the cabbage is very finely shredded – the coleslaw is often used in sandwiches and rolls so it must not be difficult to eat – then mix it with the carrots and onion. Blend the mayonnaise with the yogurt and season to taste. Add the dressing to the salad and mix well, then use as required as a salad garnish or in sandwiches.

FILLED ROLLS TO BE SERVED WITH OUR CARROT AND CABBAGE CRUNCH

TRADITIONAL PLOUGHMAN'S: Cheddar or Wensleydale cheese, with salad garnish.
FISHERMAN'S SALAD: Flaked smoked trout from a local game farm, with sliced cucumber.
HANDYMAN'S ROLLS: For those who can turn their hand to anything! A slice of ham with a slice of cheese and prawn coleslaw.
EGG AND COLESLAW: A daring variation on the traditional egg and cress.
SMOKED MACKEREL: Flakes of peppered mackerel with sliced tomato and coleslaw – full of flavour.
TONGUE AND BEETROOT: Thin slices of ox tongue with finely sliced beetroot – ask for mustard or horseradish when ordering.

WOOLPACK TOASTIES

This is the toasted sandwich list from the bar – decide on your own quantities of fillings, according to how many sandwiches you are making, and which ingredients you like best.

SALAMI AND STILTON: A really tasty sandwich filled with slices of peppered salami and crumbled Stilton cheese. Ask for chopped spring onions as an optional extra.

THAI CHICKEN: Tender slices of chicken breast spread with a spiced peanut sauce, shredded carrots and celery.

CHICKEN AND GRAPE WITH CURRY SAUCE: Juicy pieces of chicken mixed with chopped green grapes and bound together in a lightly curried mayonnaise. Ask for sliced banana as an optional extra.

TOMATO, MOZZARELLA AND PESTO: The ideal sandwich for those of you who would rather be in the Mediterranean! Ripe, flavour-packed tomatoes with melting mozzarella cheese in a sandwich spread with pungent basil-flavoured pesto sauce.

AMERICAN BEEF AND PICKLES: Thin slices of pastrami, a spiced beef, on bread spread with mild mustard and topped with sliced dill pickles. Ask for sliced Swiss cheese as an optional extra.

HAWAIIAN HAM: A thick slice of tender ham, topped with a ring of pineapple, a slice of mango and a dash of chilli sauce.

DALES' CHEESE AND COLESLAW SPECIAL: A popular sandwich made with our local cheese and home-made coleslaw. Crumbled Wensleydale from a nearby creamery, topped with sliced tomatoes and our special coleslaw. A family favourite.

ALAN'S WINE BAR

There is a popular belief amongst city folk that their country-dwelling cousins live behind the times, that they don't embrace new ideas and despise words like 'progress' and 'change'. This couldn't be further from the truth. When it was first mooted on the Emmerdale grapevine that I planned to open a wine bar/bistro in The Woolpack, the Eric Pollards of this world scoffed, and claimed the idea was doomed to failure. The truth was something different; the wine bar opened, new custom came my way and Eric turned out to be one of my most frequent diners!

Frank Tate once claimed that I owed the secret of my success to a happy combination of European panache and British simplicity, and he was right, for the mainstay of all my dishes was straightforward ingredients, all freely available over here: traditional meats, fresh fruit and vegetables. I merely used a different approach to dress them up. The biggest secret of all I kept to myself, but as I am in a generous mood I will share it with you. Always remember this – however exotic your dish might sound, however delicious the sauce – always keep it simple.

BAKED CAMEMBERT

SERVES 2

This is such a simple starter to prepare, but it is unusual and very popular. It works well, even if the Camembert is slightly under-ripe. The cheese was always cut and served at the table in The Woolpack wine bar, so that the guests could see the way the cheese oozes when cut.

8oz (225g) small Camembert, ripe but not runny	*salad garnish, crusty bread and blackcurrant jam for serving*
1tbsp flaked almonds	

Preheat the oven to 200°C/400°F/Gas 6. Place the Camembert in a small ovenproof dish and scatter the top with the almonds, pressing them into the cheese rind to make them stick.

Bake the Camembert in the preheated oven for 15 minutes. Prepare the salad garnish on individual plates. Cut the cheese and serve it with fresh crusty bread and a slightly sharp blackcurrant jam .

CLASSIC COQ AU VIN

SERVES 4

There is coq au vin and chicken in red wine – this recipe is for people who like the dish 'properly done'. I choose a full-bodied red wine for cooking and make my own chicken stock from the carcass, to give extra flavour to the dish.

3½–4lb (1.6–1.8kg) chicken, jointed into 8 pieces and carcass retained	*2oz (60g) butter*
1 bay leaf	*2tbsp virgin olive oil*
3 sprigs fresh thyme	*12 shallots or button onions, peeled but left whole*
1 small piece of celery	*4oz (120g) button mushrooms*
1 piece leek skin	*1oz (30g) flour*
1–2 cloves garlic, crushed	*salt and freshly ground black pepper to taste*
half a bottle full-bodied red wine	*large croûtes of fried bread and freshly chopped parsley to garnish*
4oz (120g) smoked back bacon, rinded and cut into small dice	

Place the chicken joints in a suitable glass or china dish. Tie the bay leaf, thyme and celery together in the leek skin to make a bouquet garni and secure with string. Add this and the crushed garlic to the chicken and cover with the wine – add a little more than half the bottle if necessary. Cover and leave the chicken for 6–8 hours, or overnight, to marinade.

Meanwhile, make a chicken stock by boiling the chicken carcass with a little onion and carrot, some herbs and peppercorns in 3–4pt (1.7–2.3l) of water. Simmer in an open pan for about 3 hours, then strain the stock through a fine sieve when cool.

Preheat the oven to 180°C/350°F/Gas 4. Blanch the diced bacon by boiling it for 1 minute in a pan of water. Drain the bacon and dry it well. Dry the chicken pieces thoroughly on absorbent kitchen paper – this is important or they will not brown and the look of the dish will not be so good. Reserve the marinade and bouquet garni.

Heat half the butter with the olive oil in an oven-proof casserole dish, add the chicken pieces and brown well on all sides. Remove the chicken from the pan with a draining spoon and set aside. Add the bacon and shallots and cook until the shallots are browned on all sides. Return the chicken to the pan and add the bouquet garni and the red wine marinade, a little salt and pepper and sufficient chicken stock to cover the chicken pieces. Cover the casserole and cook it in the preheated oven for 1 hour, until the chicken is cooked through and tender.

Remove the chicken and onions to a serving dish and keep them warm. Skim any fat from the casserole and discard the bouquet garni. Add the button mushrooms and simmer for 3–4 minutes. Beat the flour with the remaining butter and add the mixture, a little at a time, to the pan. Whisk the sauce constantly and boil the mixture between each addition of butter and flour. Season the sauce to taste and spoon it over the chicken. Garnish the coq au vin with the fried bread and chopped parsley before serving with freshly cooked vegetables.

ROSEMARY'S TIPSY TART

SERVES 6

This is rich and heavenly! Just remember that the better the brandy, the better the mousse!

FOR THE SHORTBREAD BASE

8oz (225g) plain flour	*5$\frac{1}{2}$oz (160g) butter, at*
3oz (90g) caster sugar	*room temperature*

FOR THE CHOCOLATE MOUSSE

7oz (200g) bar good	*4 eggs, size 2, separated*
quality plain chocolate	*2tbsp brandy*

Rub the butter into the flour and sugar to make the shortbread base. Stop mixing as soon as the mixture resembles fine crumbs – it is easier to mould when at the crumb stage. Press the mixture onto the base and sides of a deep 8in (20cm) sandwich tin with a loose bottom. Chill for 30 minutes. Preheat the oven to 160°C/325°F/Gas 3. Prick the base of the shortbread with a fork and bake blind for 45 minutes, until a pale golden brown. Allow to cool.

Prepare the chocolate mousse. Melt the chocolate in the microwave or in a bowl over a pan of hot water. Cool slightly, then beat in the egg yolks and brandy. Whisk the egg whites until stiff then fold into the chocolate mixture. Pour the mousse into the shortbread case and chill for 2–3 hours before serving. Decorate with cream and chocolate curls.

Shirley, my dear departed wife, and I were like chalk and cheese. We were such complete opposites that I often wondered how we ever managed to make it down the aisle together – Jack Spratt and his wife were more compatible. When we met at her voluntary soup kitchen, I was appalled by the slapdash nature of her operation. Food was never ready on time, cutlery went missing, the serving staff often failed to turn up; every day was a disaster. When she moved in with me and started to help out in the wine bar, her informal and irreverent nature actually improved the ambience. The stuffy formality I had imbued the restaurant with soon evaporated. Tablecloths vanished and were replaced with simple mats, candles in old bottles replaced fuel-burning lamps. Shirley told me that red wine need not necessarily be drunk with red meat, nor white wine with just fish and poultry. She recommended that I decide for myself how I enjoy my food and wine – I should not be dictated to by protocol and etiquette. Thus the following dishes are dedicated to Shirley Turner who believed that good food could be cooked and eaten anytime, anywhere, and the colour of the accompanying wine mattered not, as long as it was good.

ALAN'S SPECIAL PRAWN COCKTAIL

SERVES 4

I often despair at the predictability of the average English diner. I would love to drop prawn cocktails from my menu, but I know that I would lose a lot of customers if I did. I have consoled myself by spicing up this perennial favourite.

lettuce leaves for serving – use a red-tinged lettuce if possible	1dsp freshly chopped mint
1 large dessert apple, cored and finely diced	8–10oz (225–275g) peeled prawns
lemon juice	6tbsp mayonnaise
half a small cucumber, finely diced	1tbsp tomato purée
12 seedless green grapes, halved	1tbsp curry paste
	salt and freshly ground black pepper
	4 small sprigs of mint for garnish

Shred the lettuce leaves and arrange them in the bottom of four glasses or dishes. Toss the apple in lemon juice to prevent it from browning, then mix the apple with the cucumber, grapes, mint and prawns.

Mix the mayonnaise with any remaining lemon juice, the tomato purée and the curry paste, then season the dressing to taste with salt and pepper. Pile the prawn mixture onto the lettuce then top with the curried mayonnaise. Decorate with sprigs of mint.

BURGUNDY DAUBE OF BEEF WITH OLIVES

SERVES 6

This is a traditional dish of the Burgundy area of France, so I choose a suitable Burgundy for the cooking and recommend something a little more classy to drink with it. The olives add a taste of Provençe and a little extra richness – as if it were needed! The flavour of the daube develops if it is left to stand overnight, in which case the tapenade and olives should be added at the end of reheating.

3tbsp virgin olive oil, with a good fruity flavour	1 large cinnamon stick, broken
2lb (900g) stewing steak, cut into 2in (5cm) pieces	2 bay leaves
	1 orange, grated rind
1 large onion, sliced	3 cloves garlic, crushed
8oz (225g) streaky bacon, rinded and chopped	salt and freshly ground black pepper
	1 bottle red Burgundy wine
14oz (400g) can chopped tomatoes	2–3tbsp tapenade or black olive paste
3 large carrots, thickly sliced	4oz (120g) black olives, pitted
3 large sprigs fresh thyme, or 1tsp dried	buttered tagliatelle or noodles, and freshly chopped parsley for serving
3 cloves	

Preheat the oven to 160°C/325°F/Gas 3. Heat the oil in a large flameproof casserole and brown the steak on all sides – you may need to do this in two batches. Remove the steak and set aside. Cook the onion and bacon until soft in the oil left in the casserole, then return the meat to the pan. Add all the remaining ingredients except the tapenade and the olives, using enough Burgundy to cover the meat. Cover the casserole dish and cook slowly in the preheated oven for 3 hours.

Season the daube to taste, then add the tapenade and the olives. Cook for a further 10 minutes, then serve garnished with freshly chopped parsley on a bed of buttered noodles.

WILD DUCK
with Lemon and Pear Sauce

SERVES 2–3

Wild duck has a wonderful flavour and is far less fatty than duckling. As a change from the more traditional orange or cherry sauces, I serve a tangy lemon and pear sauce with the duck. It's rather a muddy brown colour but the flavour is wonderful!

1 wild duck
juice of 3 lemons
salt and freshly ground
*   black pepper*
1 small onion, very
*   finely chopped*

1 ripe dessert pear,
*   peeled and finely sliced*
2–3tbsp brandy
sugar to taste
freshly chopped parsley
*   to garnish*

Preheat the oven to 200°C/400°F/Gas 6. Place the duck on a rack in a roasting tin, pour the juice of 2 lemons over then cook for about 1 hour. Turn the oven down low, place the duck on a plate and keep it warm until required.

Strain all but two tablespoons of fat from the tin, then place it on the hob and cook the onion in the remaining fat until soft. Add the pear, juice and rind of the remaining lemon and cook until the pear is soft. Blend to a smooth sauce in a liquidiser or food processor, or press the mixture through a metal sieve. Season the sauce to taste with salt, pepper and sugar.

Carve the duck, then serve with the sauce spooned over and garnish with chopped parsley.

PINEAPPLE AND
CARDAMOM MERINGUES

SERVES 4

Meringue nests are almost inevitable on most pub menus, so I have devised this alternative.

1 small fresh pineapple,
*   peeled, cored and cut*
*   into 4 slices*
1–2tbsp seedless raisins

4 passion fruits
6 green cardamoms
2 egg whites, size 3
4oz (120g) caster sugar

Preheat the oven to 200°C/400°F/Gas 6. Place the pineapple slices in individual ovenproof serving dishes, then fill with a mixture of the raisins and the passion fruit seeds.

Crush the cardamoms to release their seeds and discard the husks. Crush the seeds in a pestle and mortar, or with the end of a rolling pin. Whisk the egg whites until stiff, then gradually whisk in the sugar mixed with the cardamom seeds. The meringue should peak stiffly in the bowl.

Pile the meringue over the fruit in the serving dishes, ensuring that all the pineapple is hidden. Flash cook the meringues for about 10 minutes in the hot oven, then serve them immediately.

CHRISTMAS IN EMMERDALE

The festive lights of the big city and the sophisti-cated Yuletide window displays of the large department stores are no substitute for Christmas in Emmerdale. The festive season somehow seems more special – more real. A candlelit procession through the village streets, accompanied by the Emmerdale carol singers, evokes an almost Dickensian image of Christmas long gone. But you won't find anyone in Emmerdale looking wistfully back to the past, complaining that Christmas is too commercialised, for towards the end of the year the village closes its borders to the world, cosy fires are stoked and doors are opened to neighbours, friends and loved ones. Jan Glover told me that last Christmas will always be remembered as a special one in the hearts of her family; earlier that year they had lost everything – Ned's job, the farm – and for a while, living in a caravan, life seemed very bleak indeed. Even when things started to look up for them and they moved into Annie's cottage, thoughts

of Christmas filled them with dread because money was tight. Friends and neighbours rallied round: Jack Sugden presented them with a plump Emmerdale turkey; Sarah gave them one of Annie's famous Christmas puddings; and their festive drink was donated by yours truly. When the carol singers paid them a visit on Christmas Eve, Jan and Ned joined them in a tour of the village.

The Reverend Donald Hinton used to be in charge of carol singing at Christmas-time, and he organised the event with almost military precision. I have never been renowned for being in possession of a tuneful singing voice, but despite my protestations Donald always succeeded in recruiting me. 'You have a healthy set of lungs and short sturdy legs,' he'd tell me, 'we'll see you at six tomorrow evening outside the church.' One failed to turn up at one's peril. Despite the Reverend's initial cajoling I returned year after year; come hail or snow we'd brave the elements to visit outlying farmsteads. Old

Bill Whiteley, who lived alone on his bleak small-holding, would stand in his doorway, a tear in his eye, and although affectionate words had long been banished from his vocabulary, his offer of hot chocolate and Christmas cake was his way of thanking us. The older members of our choir would retire to The Woolpack at the end of the evening for mulled wine and Christmas cheer. It's pleasing to know that the tradition continues every year. Donald Hinton has moved on, but stalwarts like Caroline and Nick Bates, Kathy Tate, Jack and Sarah Sugden and myself join the young farmers as they travel from village to village, often dressed as Father Christmas and his helpers. You may not know this, but round our way Father Christmas drives a tractor, not a sledge.

On the night before Christmas St Mary's Church is filled with the sound of singing. Joy and happiness permeate through the old stone walls, enveloping the village like a warm rug.

WHISKY MAC
HOT CHOCOLATE

SERVES 2

A warming winter nightcap to see the regulars on their way home from The Woolpack. Don't vary the amounts of whisky and ginger wine too much, or the sobering effect of the chocolate will be lost!

16fl oz (460ml) milk	*2tbsp ginger wine*
2tbsp drinking chocolate	*whipped cream to serve*
4tbsp whisky	*(optional)*

Scatter the drinking chocolate over the milk in a saucepan then heat until almost boiling, whisking all the time. Cool for a minute or so, then whisk in the whisky and ginger wine. Sweeten to taste if necessary and serve in two large mugs. Top with whipped cream if you are feeling totally decadent.

CAROL SINGING

HONEYED BITE-SIZE BANGERS

ABOUT 40 SAUSAGES

A good sausage is a feast in itself – a poor one definitely needs a little help to make it more special. An attractive way of serving these sausages is in a hollowed out crusty loaf.

1½lb (680g) cocktail sausages	*freshly ground black pepper*
2tbsp clear honey	

Preheat the oven to 200°C/400°F/Gas 6. Cut the sausages into individual links and prick them lightly with a fork. Place the sausages in a roasting tin and drizzle the honey over them. Cook for 15 minutes, then turn the sausages, baste them and cook for a further 15 minutes. Season lightly with pepper then serve on cocktail sticks.

GARLIC SALMON BITES

MAKES ABOUT 30

These tasty cocktail savouries are economical to make and always popular – garlic is a winner in any shape or form for the majority of people. They may be prepared well in advance and fried when required to serve warm, but they are also delicious cold. These are good for parties but also for offering to cold carol singers.

4oz (120g) instant potato	*1 clove garlic, crushed*
16fl oz (460ml) boiling water	*1tbsp freshly chopped parsley*
½tsp salt	*2 large eggs, beaten*
knob of butter	*breadcrumbs for frying*
7½oz (212g) can salmon, drained and flaked	*oil for deep-frying*
	mayonnaise or spicy sauce for serving

Make up the instant potato as directed but using only the amount of water specified above. Add salt and butter and mix to a stiff consistency, then allow to cool.

Add the flaked salmon, garlic and chopped parsley and mix well. Form teaspoonfuls of mixture into about 30 balls, flouring your hands if necessary. Dip into beaten egg then coat with the breadcrumbs, then repeat the process for a double coating.

Heat the oil for frying in a large pan until a small piece of bread dropped into the hot oil floats immediately to the surface and browns. Cook the salmon bites in three batches for about 3–4 minutes, until golden brown. Drain well on absorbent kitchen paper before serving with mayonnaise or a spicy dipping sauce of your choice.

POST OFFICE CHRISTMAS CAKE

MAKES ONE 9IN (22.5CM) ROUND CAKE

Not everyone likes a very rich Christmas cake – this is the Windsors' recipe and all the ingredients can be bought in their shop, including the roll-out icing. When Viv has the time she cuts up the cake to make a ski scene for the children – stick the pieces of cake together with apricot jam to resemble the hills around Emmerdale, then cover the cake with marzipan (to hide all the joins) and use fondant icing for the ski slopes and fluffed-up royal icing to cover the sides of the cake.

1lb (460g) dried mixed fruit	block margarine, cut into small pieces
1/4pt (150ml) sherry	6oz (175g) demerara sugar
1lb (460g) self-raising flour, wholewheat or white, or a mixture of both	4oz (120g) glacé cherries, washed and roughly chopped
pinch of salt	4 eggs, size 3, beaten
2tsp mixed spice	1/4pt (150ml) milk (approx)
8oz (225g) butter or	

Soak the fruit in the sherry whilst preparing the rest of the cake. Preheat the oven to 180°C/350°F/Gas 4. Lightly grease and double line a 9in (22.5cm) deep cake tin.

Place the flour, salt and spice in a large bowl, add the butter and rub it into the flour until the mixture resembles fine breadcrumbs. Stir in the sugar, then add the sherry-soaked fruit and the chopped cherries. Beat the eggs with the milk and add them to the bowl, mixing to a soft dropping consistency – add extra milk if necessary. It is very important to have a soft mixture, otherwise the cake will crack during baking and be dry.

Spoon the mixture into the tin, scooping out the centre to form a slight dip. Bake in the preheated oven for about 2 hours, until the cake has stopped 'singing' (yes, go on – listen to it!) and a skewer inserted into the centre comes out clean.

Allow the cake to cool slightly then remove it from the tin. Cool completely. Cover with almond paste (8oz (225g) will just cover the top – you will need about three times as much to make a ski scene), sticking it to the cake with warmed apricot jam. Allow 3–4 days for the marzipan to dry out before icing the cake.

One 1lb (460g) packet of fondant icing will make two ski runs on a cake. Use 2 egg whites, 1lb (460g) icing sugar and 1tsp glycerine to make royal icing for the sides of the cake, fluffing it up with a fork to resemble rough snow. Decorate with ski figures and small Christmas trees. To finish the cake professionally pipe a border of royal icing around the sides of the cake board, then add a little water to any remaining royal icing and use it to 'flood' the cake board to look like snow. Cutting a ski scene cake is an interesting challenge!

FESTIVE CHERRY FUDGE

MAKES ABOUT 2LB (900G)

Homemade fudge cannot be hurried but the resulting sweets are well worth the time spent in making them. Leave out the cherries and add 1tsp vanilla essence, rather than just a few drops, if you prefer a plain fudge. Fudge freezes well but don't think that will remove the temptation to over-indulge: it's also delicious straight from the freezer!

14oz (405g) can condensed milk	few drops of vanilla essence
1/2pt (280ml) milk	4oz (120g) glacé cherries, washed and chopped
2lb (900g) granulated sugar	
4oz (120g) butter	

Butter a tin about 10x6in (25x15cm). Heat the milks, sugar and butter slowly together until the sugar has dissolved and the butter is melted, then bring the mixture to the boil, stirring all the time. Boil slowly until the soft ball stage is reached at 116°C/240°F – don't be tempted to hurry this process or the fudge might well burn. It does seem to take ages to go the last little way!

Remove the pan from the heat and add the vanilla essence and cherries immediately. Beat vigorously until the mixture thickens and becomes slightly granular, then pour it into the prepared tin. Mark into pieces when cooled, then cut when completely cold and store in an air-tight tin.

PEPPERED BAKED POTATOES

SERVES 4

Baked potatoes are welcome bar food at any time of year, but this festive filling makes them one of the most popular snacks at The Woolpack at Christmas. The goat's cheese may be omitted, or a different cheese, such as Stilton or Cheddar, can be used if preferred.

These baked potatoes may be served on their own, or with a side salad. Use a sliced onion in place of the chicory if preferred, but the chicory gives a good colour to the dish.

4 large potatoes, scrubbed and scored	*salt and freshly ground black pepper*
2tbsp olive oil	*6 large fresh basil leaves,*
1 head chicory, halved lengthways and sliced	*roughly torn, or 1tsp dried*
2 red peppers, seeded and sliced	*4 slices goat's cheese in olive oil, weighing*
2 green peppers, seeded and sliced	*about 1–2oz (30–60g) each – reserve the oil*
1 clove garlic, crushed	
8oz (225g) tomatoes, preferably peeled	

Cook the potatoes in a preheated oven at 200°C/400°F/Gas 6 for about 1½ hours, or until cooked.

Prepare the stewed peppers while the potatoes are baking. Heat the oil in a frying-pan, add the chicory and cook until soft. Stir in the prepared peppers and the garlic, cook for a few minutes to soften the peppers slightly, then add the tomatoes and the seasonings. Cover the pan and cook slowly for 30 minutes, until the peppers are soft but not mushy. Season to taste.

Preheat the grill. Cut the potatoes in half and place each one in a heatproof serving dish. Spoon the peppers over the potatoes, then top with rounds of goat's cheese.

Grill quickly until the cheese is slightly browned, then drizzle with the oil from the cheese and serve immediately.

WINTER SUNSHINE SAVOURIES

MAKES 16

Devils on Horseback, prunes wrapped in bacon, are always popular party nibbles but, if the prunes are not already pitted, they are time-consuming to prepare. Sun dried tomatoes are not available in the Windsor's shop but I can get them through the wholesalers. They make a delicious alternative to prunes, and are much quicker to prepare as a savoury snack.

8 rashers streaky bacon, rind removed	*freshly ground black pepper*
16 sun dried tomatoes in oil, drained	

Preheat the oven to 200°C/400°F/Gas 6. Stretch the rashers of bacon with the back of a knife, then cut them into two. Wrap each piece around a tomato and secure the bacon in place with a wooden cocktail stick. Season lightly with pepper.

Bake on a baking sheet in the preheated oven for 10–12 minutes, until the bacon is browned. Cool slightly before serving – the tomatoes get very hot!

SPECIAL MINCEMEAT AND WALNUT STRUDEL

MAKES 16 SLICES

When trade is brisk at Christmas there simply isn't time in The Woolpack's kitchen to roll out enough pastry for all the mince pies that are required. These strudels slice up well and can be made very quickly when news of the carol singers reaches the pub.

4 large sheets of filo pastry	*2oz (60g) walnut pieces, chopped*
2oz (60g) butter, melted	*icing sugar for dredging*
8tbsp mincemeat	

Preheat the oven to 190°C/375°F/Gas 5. Lay out two sheets of the pastry and brush them with melted butter. Cover with the remaining sheets and brush again.

Spread one lot of pastry with half the mincemeat, then scatter with half the nuts. Top with the remaining pair of pastry sheets, then spread them with the remaining mincemeat and nuts.

Fold the two short sides in over the edge of the filling, brush with butter then fold up one of the long sides. Keep rolling to give a long strudel roll, and brush the last edge of the pastry with butter to seal the strudel.

Place the roll on a baking sheet, bending it slightly if necessary. Bake in the preheated oven for 15–20 minutes until golden brown, then dredge with sieved icing sugar before cutting into slices and serving.

ST CLEMENT'S MINCE PIES

The Woolpack's mince pies are really special – tangy and not too rich. Be sure to pot the mincemeat in warm, sterile jars and store in a cool place for 2–3 weeks before use. I always use vegetarian suet so that the mincemeat is suitable for everyone. The short, buttery homemade pastry has a slight hint of orange in it which complements the citrus flavour of St Clement's mincemeat perfectly.

FOR THE MINCEMEAT *(ABOUT 3LB/1.4KG)*

1lb (460g) cooking apples, peeled and sliced	1 lemon
	1 orange
8oz (225g) sultanas	1tsp ground cinnamon
8oz (225g) seedless raisins	1tsp ground nutmeg
	1tsp ground cloves
8oz (225g) chopped peel	6oz (175g) vegetarian suet
8oz (225g) light Muscovado sugar	3tbsp Cointreau or Grand Marnier

Stew the apples with as little water as possible and no sugar. Pour the apple into a large mixing bowl and beat until smooth, then allow to cool completely.

Add all the remaining ingredients, adding both the grated rind and the juice from the lemon and orange. Stir thoroughly, then cover and leave overnight.

Warm some sterile jars in the oven. Stir the mincemeat and spoon it into the warm jars, packing it down firmly with a spoon to exclude any air which might cause the mincemeat to deteriorate. Cover and seal. Allow to mature for 2–3 weeks before using.

FOR THE PASTRY *(MAKES 24 PIES)*

12oz (340g) plain flour	8oz (225g) butter, cut into small pieces
2oz (60g) caster sugar	
1 orange, grated rind and juice	1 egg, size 3, beaten

Preheat the oven to 190°C/375°F/Gas 5 and lightly butter two trays of patty tins. Mix the flour and sugar together, then add the grated orange rind. Rub in the butter until the mixture resembles fine breadcrumbs and bind with the beaten egg. (The butter and egg may be added together if the pastry is made in a mixer or processor.)

Roll out the pastry, cut out 48 circles with a fluted pastry cutter and use half to line the patty tins. Fill with a heaped teaspoonful of mincemeat then cover each pie with a pastry lid, moistening it with the orange juice to stick. Brush the pies with any remaining orange juice and bake for 20–25 minutes in the preheated oven. Dredge lightly with caster sugar when cooked, then allow the pies to cool slightly in the tins before removing them to a wire rack to cool completely.

ALAN'S CHRISTMAS WARMER

SERVES 20

Mulled wine can be a disaster! There is an overwhelming temptation to put just about everything into one brew, resulting in a mess of flavours which actually taste of nothing except an elaborate plot to disguise a bottle of cheap wine! This recipe is very simple and delicious – cranberry juice is widely available in grocers and supermarkets.

2½pt (1.5l) red wine	2 cinnamon sticks, broken
1¾pt (1l) orange juice	
1¾pt (1l) cranberry juice	4oz (120g) demerara sugar
6 cloves	1 orange

Place all the ingredients in a large pan and heat them gently until very hot – allow about 20 minutes for the flavours to blend together really well.

Cut the ends from the orange, then cut it into quarters and slice very thinly before adding to the pan. Ladle into heatproof goblets or cups to serve.

THE WOOLPACK AT CHRISTMAS

I always look forward to Christmas at The Woolpack. Several colleagues of mine in the licensed pub trade refuse to open up for the Christmas Day lunchtime pub session; they say they would rather be at home with their families. I agree with the sentiment, but as I look upon my clientèle as family it seems only fitting that I open my doors and share the day with them. Homemade hot mince pies and mulled wine go down a treat, so much so that when it's time to ask people to leave at the end of the afternoon, it takes much persuasion to make them return to their loved ones!

I am proud to belong to the extended family of The Woolpack. I hope that the happiness and joy I derive from being landlord is reciprocated by my customers. Once a year, at Christmas, I like to show my appreciation of their patronage by hosting a special luncheon for older regulars, the needy and the infirm. Delicious traditional fare is accompanied by song and dance – usually Seth at the piano! Amos and Mr Wilks used to donate Christmas hampers to their older regulars. I prefer to cook them a dinner they'll never forget – and as they come back to me year after year, I think I'm doing the right thing!

AVOCADO AND STILTON DIP

SERVES 4–6 AS A STARTER

Stilton and walnuts are traditional foods of Christmas – blend them with creamy avocados and a little garlic and you have a wonderful dip cum vegetarian pâté cum seasonal salad dressing. To keep the bright green colour of the dip do not make it too far in advance of serving, or the avocados may discolour. This is particularly delicious when served as a dip if bacon-flavoured crisps are used for dipping.

2 medium avocados, stoned and peeled	2–3tbsp soured cream
1 clove garlic, crushed	salt and freshly ground black pepper
2oz (60g) Stilton	1oz (30g) walnuts

Place all the ingredients except the nuts and seasoning in a liquidiser or food processor and blend until smooth. Season to taste, then transfer to a serving dish. Stir in the walnuts and serve.

BOXING DAY SALAD

SERVES 4

When recovering from the rich food of Christmas, a salad can make a very welcome change. This salad contains lots of seasonal foods and is filling in itself, but has a goodly amount of crispy vegetables to exercise the teeth and the digestive system!

red, white and green salad leaves	3oz (90g) Stilton cheese, cut into wafer-thin slivers
14oz (400g) can flageolet beans, drained and rinsed	1½oz (45g) pecan nuts or walnuts
8 small flavoursome tomatoes, quartered	2oz (60g) garlic-flavoured croûtons
6oz (175g) cooked ham	5–6tbsp vinaigrette dressing
8oz (225g) cooked chicken	

Prepare the salad either in a serving dish or on individual plates. Arrange the flageolet beans on a bed of the mixed lettuce leaves, then top with all the remaining ingredients. Dress with a well-flavoured vinaigrette, toss lightly and serve.

HARROGATE ORANGE AND ALMOND TRIFLE

SERVES 6

You can't beat a trifle when it comes to producing a pudding that is to appeal to everyone! This one has a touch of luxury about it – ratafias for the base, a generous splash of liqueur and a delicious homemade orange-flavoured custard. Festive and refreshing!

4oz (120g) ratafia biscuits or broken macaroons	3tbsp Grand Marnier or Cointreau
11oz (300g) can mandarins, drained and syrup reserved	1pt (570ml) milk
1 orange, pared rind and juice	4 eggs, beaten
5oz (142g) tablet orange jelly	2oz (60g) caster sugar
½pt (280ml) boiling water (approx)	2tsp cornflour
	¼pt (150ml) double cream, whipped
	toasted flaked almonds, for decoration

Place the biscuits in the base of a glass trifle dish and add the mandarin segments. Add the juice from the can to the jelly segments with the juice of the fresh orange, then make the mixture up to 1pt (570ml) with boiling water. Stir until the jelly is dissolved then cool slightly before adding the liqueur of your choice. Pour the jelly over the biscuits and leave until cool, then refrigerate until set.

Meanwhile, heat the pared orange rind with the milk until the milk is almost boiling. Remove the pan from the heat, cover and leave for at least 20 minutes, to allow the rind to flavour the milk.

Strain the milk and discard the orange zest. Whisk together the eggs, sugar and cornflour. Reheat the milk until almost boiling, then whisk it into the egg mixture. Reheat the custard, stirring continuously, until it is just thick enough to coat the back of a wooden spoon – don't overcook the mixture or the eggs will scramble and curdle the custard! Whisk thoroughly, then set aside to cool slightly. Whisk again (don't leave it long enough for a skin to form), then pour the custard over the set jelly. Allow to cool then chill until the custard is set, in about 2 hours.

Decorate the trifle with whipped cream and toasted flaked almonds before serving.

Hotten Spicy

One cold spring morning, several years ago, Amos Brearly was brushing down the forecourt of The Woolpack, a task he carried out daily with almost religious fervour; a tidy pub forecourt was of the utmost importance to him. But I digress. There was something different about this morning. Or rather, something different happened. Amos saw something he shouldn't have seen.

Stopping in his task to wipe his brow, his gaze turned upwards to the bedroom window of the house opposite. Mrs Bates' cottage as it was then – nowadays it's occupied by Eric Pollard. What he saw there made him turn pale. A large, shameless, middle-aged man was getting dressed in full view of the street. This awful vision sent Amos scurrying back into the safety of the pub. Apart from recounting the tale to Mr Wilks, his partner, Amos kept this story to himself. Caroline Bates' indiscretion remains a secret to this day. How did I come to hear of it, you might ask? Not from Amos. Haven't you guessed? I was the large man dressing in the bedroom window (I happened to be engaged to Caroline at the time).

I use this story to illustrate a point. And that is, the landlord of a hostelry, especially in a small village, overhears and observes most things that are going on, for the pub is the centre of the village universe. But knowing about them, and talking about them, are two different things. And I like to think that I carry on Amos's discreet code of honour. I see certain things and I hear certain things…but I only ever discuss them amongst my closest friends!

Of course, there have been times when my attempts at discretion have proved pointless; certain members of the community have used The Woolpack to broadcast their problems to the world. Take the Tate family, for instance. Frank's on the wagon now (I know how he feels) but when he threw Kim out for her dalliance with Neil Kincaid, he more or less moved in to the bar full-time. One drunken evening he bumped into his wife and called her all sorts of terrible names. We were all left with no doubts as to what had been going on in that household.

Lynn Whiteley was always courting controversy in The Woolpack. I breathed a sigh of relief when she announced her decision to leave the area. She's in Australia now with her sheep-shearer friend. Best place for her. I lost track of the number of times she ended up with a drink thrown in her face. Sarah Sugden, who isn't well known for public disturbances, threw a gin and tonic at her. Something to do with Lynn setting her sights on Jack, I think. Then Rachel tipped a drink over her. Something to do with Lynn's interest in Joe, I gather. I was annoyed with Rachel – she was working behind the bar for me at the time. Call me old-fashioned, but I like my employees to serve the customers properly – and that means serving drinks in glasses, not hurling them across the bar top. So Lynn has gone but life is far from quiet. Luke McAllister's love life and the feud with the Dingles is the source of constant gossip, Rachel's relationship with Christopher Tate has raised a few eyebrows and my own confrontations with the devious Eric Pollard have given people something to talk about too!

I think Lynn Whiteley would be proud of us all.

EMMERDALE FARM

Earlier in their relationship Sarah Sugden's culinary skills were a source of great amusement to Jack. Her cakes always turned out flat and hard and her stews dry. At one point, when the jibing became too great, she threw in the towel and handed back the kitchen apron to Annie. However, a few lessons with Annie and Sarah's cooking was no longer a joke. When Annie decided to call it a day at Emmerdale Sarah decided that she and Jack should be equally responsible for the cooking. As you can imagine this was not very well received by Jack, who was of the belief that a man's place was in the field behind the wheel of a tractor, not in the kitchen beside a cooker. A few cookery lessons and several arguments later, Jack was able to serve up a stew and whip up a dessert even Ma would have been proud of. Now that Sarah is a working mother Jack is happy to prepare meals for the family. The following recipes from the Sugden household are delicious, uncomplicated and easy to prepare; and even Jack can now see that having a microwave means that he doesn't have to wait too long for his dinner.

BRAISED RED CABBAGE

SERVES 3–4

Sarah really has to think hard about when to use her microwave – having an Aga at Hawthorn Cottage she always has a cooker ready to cook. Red cabbage is one of her favourite microwave dishes – it is cooked in 15 minutes and maintains a gloriously vibrant red colour, whereas cooked conventionally it takes at least 1 hour, and often takes on a dark, muddy appearance.

1oz (30g) butter
8oz (225g) red cabbage, finely shredded
1 Granny Smith dessert apple, peeled, cored and sliced
1 small onion, finely sliced
1tsp caraway seeds
2 bay leaves
1tbsp demerara sugar
salt and freshly ground black pepper
3tbsp red wine vinegar

Heat the butter for 1 minute on full power in a microwave casserole dish, then stir in the cabbage, cover and cook for 4 minutes, stirring once. If the cabbage is well coated in the melted butter it will cook evenly.

Add all the remaining ingredients and stir well. Cook for a further 10 minutes with the dish covered, and stir half way through cooking.

Stand for 3 or 4 minutes, then stir again, season to taste and serve.

TRAWLERMAN'S PATE

SERVES 6

This pâté may be made with either kippers or smoked mackerel but Sarah prefers to use kippers as she feels they have a better flavour. Either fish combines well with horseradish for a really well-seasoned pâté. Cooking the fish in the microwave prevents the smell from getting all around the house.

1lb (460g) kipper fillets	1 spring onion, very
7oz (200g) cream cheese	finely chopped
1–2tbsp horseradish	freshly ground black
sauce	pepper

Cook the kipper fillets in a covered microwave dish for 4–5 minutes on full power. Leave to cool, then skin and flake the fish, removing any obvious bones.

Beat the cream cheese until soft, then add the horseradish, spring onion and the flaked kippers. Mix well – to make a smooth pâté you may blend the mixture in a liquidiser or food processor. Season to taste with black pepper, then turn into a serving dish and chill until required. Serve with hot buttered toast.

QUICK PRAWN CURRY

SERVES 4

All prawn curries are quick to cook but the smell of the curry can linger long after the final mouthful has been savoured when cooked in a pan on the hotplate. This curry is an excellent microwave recipe.

1 large onion	1oz (30g) creamed
1 clove garlic	coconut, crumbled
1 lime, grated rind and	1/2tsp salt
juice	1tbsp demerara sugar
3tbsp oil	1lb (460g) frozen
1tbsp curry paste	prawns
1–2tbsps tomato purée	

Roughly chop the onion, then blend it to a purée in a liquidiser or food processor with the garlic, lime zest and juice.

Stir the mixture into the oil in a large microwave dish, add the curry paste and tomato purée then cover and cook for 4 minutes on full power, stirring once. Stir in the salt, coconut and demerara sugar, then add the frozen prawns. Cover and cook for a further 4–5 minutes, stirring once. Add extra salt if necessary, stand for 2–3 minutes then serve with naan bread or rice.

SIMPLY WICKED PEARS

SERVES 4

The microwave cooks fruit beautifully without the need to add extra water, which is a great advantage when the fruit is to be served in a lovely chocolate sauce, and no extra liquid is required. Melting chocolate in the microwave is much easier than melting it in a bowl over a pan of water. This sauce is also delicious over ice cream – it's a favourite at Emmerdale Farm on any special occasion.

4 Conference or other	knob of butter
cooking pears, peeled	2tbsp clear honey
and cored	1/4 pt (150ml) single
juice of 1 lemon	cream
3 1/2oz (100g) plain	
chocolate	

Try to cut the cores out of the pears from the bottom, so that they can sit upright in a dish for serving. Place the pears with the lemon juice in a suitable dish, cover and cook for 5–6 minutes on 70% power, or until the pears are just tender. You may need to turn the pears once during cooking. Discard the lemon juice and place the pears in individual serving dishes.

Break the chocolate into pieces and melt it with the butter and honey by heating on full power for 2–3 minutes – stir the chocolate during this period to check that it is melting evenly. Add the cream and stir well, then heat for a further 1 minute. Pour the sauce over the pears and serve.

FARMER'S WINTRY WARMER

SERVES 4

A microwave cooker can be disastrous for any would-be dieter with a sweet tooth in the winter – steamed puddings in minutes are perfectly possible.

3tbsp golden syrup	2 eggs, size 3, beaten
4oz (120g) soft	1tsp baking powder
margarine	1tsp ground ginger
4oz (120g) self-raising	2–3tbsp warm water
flour	2oz (60g) sultanas
4oz (120g) caster sugar	

Lightly grease a 2pt (1.14l) pudding basin and spoon the golden syrup into the bottom of the bowl. Place all the remaining ingredients in a large bowl and beat thoroughly, either with a wooden spoon or an electric mixer, until smooth and creamy. Add the water to give a very soft dropping consistency (the mixture should literally 'splat' off the spoon) then fold in the sultanas.

Spoon the mixture into the prepared bowl then smooth the top. Cook the pudding on 70% power, preferably on a rack, for 6 minutes, until it is just starting to shrink away from the sides of the bowl.

Leave the pudding to stand for at least 5 minutes, then turn it out and serve with custard.

Before taking stock of her life and deciding that she needed a change, Annie Sugden's taste was traditional and conservative, especially when it came to food. Nowadays it's a different story; moving to Spain has widened her horizons and made her more amenable to new culinary experiences. Sadly the same can't be said of Jack. The Sugden boys were brought up on a diet of traditional stews, roasts and casseroles, and even today Jack would really prefer a lamb stew to spaghetti bolognaise. Sarah, when it is her turn to prepare supper, has picked up the challenge and is determined to educate her husband's palate. Sarah is no stranger to the exotic: several years ago after leaving college she took time off and backpacked around the world, visiting India, Malaysia, Thailand and Japan. Her cooking reflects the different cultures she experienced along the way. She uses exotic spices and herbs to liven up the most traditional of dishes. Give them a try – you'll be mildly surprised!

MOROCCAN LAMB

SERVES 6

This is a good compromise between Jack's traditional taste for a simple lamb casserole with beans and Sarah's willingness to experiment with spices and flavourings.

8oz (225g) chick peas, soaked overnight	*1tsp ground coriander*
2tbsp olive oil	*2tsp paprika*
2 large leeks, trimmed and sliced	*salt and freshly ground black pepper*
2lb (900g) boneless lamb, shoulder or leg, diced	*1pt (570ml) stock*
	1tbsp tomato purée
	4oz (120g) seedless raisins

Preheat the oven to 180°C/350°F/Gas 4. Cook the chick peas in boiling water for 10 minutes, then drain them and keep until required. Cook the leeks in the oil in a flameproof casserole – cook slowly until they are soft but not browned. Stir in the meat, increase the heat and brown the meat all over. Add the spices, chick peas and seasoning, then stir in the stock and tomato purée. Bring the lamb to the boil, cover the casserole then transfer it to the preheated oven for 1¼ hours.

Stir the raisins into the casserole and cook for a further 15 minutes. Season to taste before serving. Rice or pasta make good accompaniments to this delicious casserole.

LIVER & BACON CASSEROLE

SERVES 4

Liver and bacon is seldom popular with children but Sarah's method of casseroling means that the whole family will enjoy this dish.

3tbsp oil	*¾pt (430ml) well-flavoured stock*
2 large onions, finely sliced	*salt and freshly ground black pepper*
1½lb (680g) lamb's liver, thinly sliced	*4 rashers back bacon, rinded*
2tbsp seasoned flour	
1 small swede, diced	

Preheat the oven to 180°C/350°F/Gas 4. Fry the onions in the oil in a flameproof casserole dish over a medium heat until they are well browned. Toss the liver in the seasoned flour, then add it to the onions and brown on all sides. Stir in the swede, then gradually add the stock, stirring up any meat sediment from the bottom of the casserole. Bring to the boil, season then cover and cook in the preheated oven for 30 minutes.

Stir the casserole, then lay the bacon over the top of the dish, cover and cook for a further 30 minutes. Season to taste, then serve with mashed potatoes and freshly cooked green vegetables.

CHICKEN ITALIA

SERVES 4

Sarah tries hard to get Jack to try new flavours and foods but his favourite remains beef stew. If she calls this Chicken and Tomato Casserole it meets with less resistance, but it has a wonderful flavour of Italy and warm, sunny days.

2tbsp fruity olive oil	*14oz (400g) can chopped*
1oz (30g) butter	*tomatoes*
8 chicken thighs, skinned	*6–8 fresh basil leaves*
2 onions, sliced	*salt and freshly ground*
1–2 cloves garlic, crushed	*black pepper*
¼pt (150ml) dry white	*¼pt (150ml) stock*
wine	*(approx)*
2 large courgettes,	
trimmed and thickly	
sliced	

FOR THE GARNISH (optional)

1tbsp each freshly	*zested rind of 1 lemon*
chopped parsley and	*(use a zester to remove*
basil	*the rind in strips)*
1–2 cloves garlic, very	
finely chopped	

Preheat the oven to 180°C/350°F/Gas 4. Heat the oil and butter together in a flameproof casserole, add the chicken and brown on both sides. Remove the chicken from the pan, add the onion and garlic and cook slowly until soft. Pour the wine into the pan, bring to the boil whilst scraping up any sediment from the bottom of the pan, and boil until reduced.

Return the chicken to the pan with the courgettes and the chopped tomatoes. Add the basil leaves, torn into pieces, salt and pepper and sufficient stock to just cover the meat. Cover the casserole and transfer to the preheated oven for 1–1¼ hours, or until the chicken is tender.

Season the casserole to taste, then serve with boiled rice or pasta.

Mix the ingredients for the garnish together and scatter a little over each helping.

I t took a long time for Sarah to get used to the ways of the countryside. A city dweller by birth, she was shocked by some of the 'backward' (her word) and seemingly barbaric farming methods used by Jack. She objected to sheep-shearing, felt sorry for the geese, sympathised with the dairy herd. She was surprised to learn that a bartering system was alive and well in North Yorkshire. Jack would loan the Emmerdale tractor to Billy Wardell, a neighbouring farmer, for the afternoon in exchange for a pork joint: a big bag of new potatoes would be exchanged for a few Emmerdale chickens. The Sugdens aren't entirely self-sufficient, but this handy local system allows them to eat fresh meat and vegetables without having to set foot in the Windors' shop for days at a time. Those of you who live in the city need not worry; the ingredients for Jack and Sarah's recipes can be easily obtained at any supermarket – in exchange for cash, of course.

SARAH'S SPECIAL SHEPHERD'S PIE

SERVES 4

Sarah adds all sorts of things to Shepherd's Pie to make it a little more exciting.

1tbsp oil	*14oz (400g) can*
1 large onion, finely	*chopped tomatoes*
sliced	*salt and freshly ground*
1lb (460g) cooked lamb,	*black pepper*
diced	*1 5-serving packet*
1tbsp freshly chopped	*instant potato*
mixed herbs, or 1tsp	*2–3oz (60–90g)*
dried	*Cheddar cheese,*
15oz (439g) can butter	*grated*
beans, drained	

Preheat the oven to 200°C/400°F/Gas 6. Cook the onion in the oil until soft then add the lamb and cook quickly to heat through. Stir in the herbs, butter beans and tomatoes, season with salt and pepper, then bring to the boil and simmer.

Make up the potato as directed, adding a little salt and butter. Transfer the lamb to an ovenproof casserole, then top with the mash and the grated cheese. Bake for 40–45 minutes, until the topping is golden brown.

EMMERDALE SUNDAY ROAST CHICKEN
with Nutty Sweetcorn and Almond Stuffing

SERVES 4–6

Roast chicken is always a winner but the stuffing can sometimes let the bird down. Sarah got the idea for this American-style stuffing from one of the glossy magazines – it works really well and the ingredients are always to hand in the store cupboard.

1 large chicken, about
   4–4¹/₂lb (1.8–2kg)
4oz (120g) fresh brown
   breadcrumbs
2oz (60g) ground
   almonds

salt and freshly ground
   black pepper
1 small onion, finely
   chopped
15oz (425g) can
   creamed sweetcorn

Preheat the oven to 190°C/375°F/Gas 5. Remove any excess fat from the chicken. Mix together all the ingredients for the stuffing and use the mixture to fill the cavity of the chicken.

Roast the chicken in the preheated oven allowing 30 minutes per 1lb (460g).

Jack's early intransigence in matters culinary, and the problems it caused for his relationship, were at the forefront of Sarah's mind when she determined to educate Robert in the ways of the kitchen at an early age. He used to love watching her and was anxious to learn, keen to dip his hands in flour and mix ingredients in a pudding basin. Sarah keeps the recipe simple and some of the cooking is done in the microwave. She suspects Robert has inherited his Grandmother's cooking skills. And it has even given Jack food for thought – if a youngster like Robert can cook for the family, then so can he!

CRISPY COD BAKE

SERVES 4

This is the type of dish that Robert enjoys cooking, and it is very useful to Sarah to have a helper in the kitchen when she is working. Robert likes to put crushed crisps on top of the dish when it is finished – he also likes to nibble one or two before he crushes them up with a rolling pin.

4 frozen cod steaks, weighing 4–6oz (120–175g) each	1tbsp tomato purée
4 tomatoes	1 slice cooked ham or 2 rashers cooked bacon, chopped
4oz (120g) Cheddar cheese, grated	1¹/₂oz (40g) packet crisps, crushed

Preheat the oven to 200°C/400°F/Gas 6. Place the cod steaks, still frozen, in a single layer in an ovenproof dish. Cut the tomatoes in half and arrange them around the outside of the fish. Mix together the cheese, tomato purée and ham or bacon and spoon over the fish. Bake in the preheated oven for 30–40 minutes. Garnish with crushed crisps and serve with freshly cooked vegetables and mashed potatoes.

MUSHROOM TWIRLS

SERVES 4

Robert uses a leek in this recipe as it is easier to cut than an onion and doesn't make him cry so easily!

2tbsp olive oil	8oz (225g) mushrooms, sliced
1 medium leek, finely sliced	14oz (400g) can chopped tomatoes
1 clove garlic, crushed	
12oz–1lb (340–460g) freshly cooked pasta twirls	salt and pepper
	grated Parmesan cheese for serving

Cook the leek in the oil until soft but not browned, then add the garlic and the mushrooms and cook for 2–3 minutes until the mushrooms are starting to soften. Add the chopped tomatoes with a little seasoning and simmer the sauce for 30 minutes, until reduced and thickened.

Serve the sauce tossed through freshly cooked pasta twirls, topped with Parmesan cheese.

STICKY SYRUP TART

SERVES 4

Lots of people say that treacle tart is difficult to make but when it is one of your favourite foods, as for Robert, it is worth persevering! Sarah has taught him to measure the syrup correctly, which is most of the battle – dip the spoon into the tin, then scrape the flat blade of a knife along the top and underside to remove any excess syrup. Too much will make the tart stodgy.

4oz (120g) plain flour	2oz (60g) fresh white breadcrumbs
2oz (60g) butter or hard margarine	6tbsp golden syrup
cold water to mix	1 lemon, grated rind

Preheat the oven to 200°C/400°F/Gas 6 then begin by making the pastry. Place the flour in a bowl. Cut the butter into tiny pieces then add it to the fat and rub it into the flour between your fingertips until the mixture looks like breadcrumbs. Add a little cold water to the mixture, about 1tbsp, and start mixing, adding more water until the pastry comes into a firm ball. This is easiest to do with a fork.

Knead the pastry lightly on a floured surface until it is a smooth ball, then roll it out to fit a 7in (17.5cm) sandwich tin. If you turn the pastry round on the work surface after every second roll it is unlikely to stick while you are rolling. Remember to push the pastry well into the corners of the tin to stop it shrinking back during cooking.

Mix together the breadcrumbs, syrup and grated lemon rind (don't grate any of the white pith with the rind or the flavour will be bitter). Spoon the mixture into the pastry case and smooth the top.

Bake the treacle tart for about 20–25 minutes in the hot oven, until golden brown. The treacle will become very hot so allow the tart to cool a little before eating it with custard.

ROBERT'S CHEWY CHOCOLATE CHIP ICE CREAM

SERVES 6–8

Designer ice creams are very expensive to buy so Sarah has encouraged Robert to make his own! This is his favourite – it is simple to make if you use canned custard as the base.

15oz (425g) can custard
¹/4pt (150ml) thick natural yogurt (slightly sweetened if possible)
¹/2pt (280ml) whipping cream
3¹/2oz (100g) toffees
2oz (50g) chocolate

Place the custard in a large mixing bowl and stir in the yogurt. Whip the cream in a separate bowl until thick but not stiff, then use a wire whisk to add the cream to the custard – add the cream to the custard and not the custard to the cream, or you will knock all the air out of the mixture.

Chop the toffees into slivers, or place them in a strong bag and hit them with a rolling pin until broken. Chop the chocolate into slivers as well and stir both into the cream mixture.

Turn into a freezer box and freeze for about 3 hours until firm, stirring once or twice to prevent large ice crystals from forming. Remove the ice cream from the freezer 20–30 minutes before serving to make it easier to scoop.

LEMON REFRESHER

SERVES 4

Homemade lemonade is much more refreshing than any you can buy.

3 large lemons
4oz (120g) caster sugar
1¹/2pt (850ml) boiling water
ice cubes for serving (optional)

Wash the lemons then pare off the rind very thinly – this means taking away just the yellow part of the lemon where all the flavour is in the skin. The easiest way to do this is by dragging a lemon zester over the surface of the fruit. Place the rind in a bowl with the sugar and add the boiling water. Stir until the sugar has dissolved, then leave to stand for 1 hour.

Add the lemon juice then strain the lemonade through a sieve to remove the rind and any pips. Chill the lemonade in the fridge and serve with ice. The lemonade will keep for 1–2 days.

Hotten Steamy

The Sugdens have only lived in their 'new' farmhouse for a relatively short period of time. However, the farmland they own has been in the family for generations. In fact there is a mention of the Sugdens and their acreage in the Domesday Book – quite impressive! Although it must hearten Jack to know that he is carrying on the age-old family tradition, the pressures on him to keep the farm in order, ready for the next generation of Sugdens to take over, must be great. Like most farmers today, he's only just managing to keep his head above water.

Over the years they've had more than their fair share of ups and downs – the volatile nature of the Sugden brothers' personalities accounts for a lot of their scrapes – Joe and Jack were both stubborn, fiery and quick to resort to using their fists when argument failed. The onset of maturity has seen them settle down but they still retain their fire and passion. Jack was distraught after the death of his first wife Pat. The sadness and the memories drove him away from Emmerdale for a while and he went to live abroad. When he returned he met Sarah Connolly and now seems quite content with his lot. Sarah, Robert and their baby, Victoria, mean the world to him. I think Sarah's independent spirit causes him some concern – she never was content just to be the farmer's wife but relationships are all

about 'give and take'. As long as Sarah can do her own thing and doesn't feel stifled by life on the farm they'll be fine. I suspect they were a couple who were always meant to be together. The news that they were getting married came as quite a surprise – it floored the village gossips who were unprepared for it. Jack and Sarah were the world's happiest unmarried couple. It was a well known fact that once a year, on the anniversary of their getting together, Jack would propose to Sarah and Sarah would refuse. Their wedding came at a time when the village needed cheering – it was a happy day for us all.

One person was not expected to attend the wedding and that was Marian Wilks, daughter of Henry Wilks. For a long time Jack was in love with Marian. Their on-off relationship went on for several years. Even after Jack and Sarah were together, I daresay. I was around when Jack called in on Henry at The Woolpack to ask for advice – Marian had called from Italy – she needed his help. Jack was living with Sarah at the time and Henry reminded him of that. Jack did indeed go to Italy but only to tell Marian that there was no future for them. He was in love with Sarah. I know they've had their ups and downs since then – in fact I did hear that Sarah left Jack for a short time last year but she soon returned. That's life though. You take the rough with the smooth.

Life at Emmerdale Farm has changed over the years. Gone are the days when old

Sam Pearson sat by the fireside moaning about his grandsons while Annie prepared dinner for Matt, Jack and Joe. Annie has moved to Spain. Poor Joe, who joined her there in an attempt to start a new life for himself, has been tragically killed in a car crash. But Jack knows that Annie will come home one day – after all, he tried to stay away and failed. Emmerdale Farm and the Sugdens are inseparable!

SHROVE TUESDAY PANCAKE DASH

Shrove Tuesday was one of those days set aside for and enjoyed by children, or so I believed until I moved to Emmerdale. How strange, I thought, on overhearing my neighbours talking excitedly about Shrove Tuesday one Monday evening in The Woolpack. The next day I was staggered to see half the village in Wellingtons running down the main street, while at the same time tossing pancakes in large frying-pans. Strange customs abound in the countryside! Never to be outdone I entered the competition the following year – and lost. I concluded that I was not cut out for pancake tossing. Nowadays the competition takes place in Hotten and people come from far and wide to join in – it has become the London Marathon of pancake races. I prefer to stick to what I'm best at – cooking and eating them. Just remember though, the secret to a good pancake is piping hot oil and light airy batter.

BASIC PANCAKE BATTER

MAKES ABOUT 8 LARGE PANCAKES

This basic batter can be made either in a liquidiser or in a bowl, with a whisk or a wooden spoon – the younger people in Emmerdale go for the technological approach whilst Betty and her contempories don't understand the need to make so much washing up!

4oz (120g) plain flour	*$\frac{1}{2}$pt (280ml) milk, or*
pinch of salt	*milk and water mixed*
1 egg, size 3	*oil for frying*

In a liquidiser: Mix the flour and salt together. Place the egg and the milk in the liquidiser goblet and process until blended. With the machine still running add the flour through the lid or down the feed tube, and continue mixing until a smooth batter is formed.
By hand: Mix the flour and salt together in a bowl then make a well in the centre. Beat the egg and drop it into the well then add the milk. Gradually whisk or beat the flour into the liquid and beat to a smooth batter.

Heat a frying-pan until it is evenly hot then add a little oil to the pan, to coat the bottom evenly. Pour in 2–3 tablespoons of the batter and spread it quickly and evenly over the pan by shaking the pan gently. Cook over a medium heat, loosening the edges of the pancake whilst it is cooking with a palette knife. Turn or toss the pancake and briefly cook the second side. Serve the pancakes hot with lemon juice and granulated sugar.

Many children take part in the Emmerdale Pancake Dash. So often pancakes are a favourite food of children when they are just learning to cook, and they usually prefer them with a sweet filling. Here is a selection of fillings from Robert Sugden and his friends.

BANANA AND MAPLE SYRUP PANCAKES

SERVES 4

1 quantity of basic	*juice of $\frac{1}{2}$ a lemon*
pancake batter	*1–2tbsp seedless raisins*
4 large bananas, peeled	*4–6tbsp maple syrup*

Mash the bananas with the lemon juice and add the raisins – add a little brown sugar if you want to but remember that the maple syrup is quite sweet.

Cook the pancakes as directed, then spread each one with a spoonful of the banana mixture and roll them up. Place on serving plates and spoon the maple syrup over the pancakes before serving.

RASPBERRIES WITH ICE CREAM

SERVES 4

1 quantity of basic	*3–4tbsp caster sugar*
pancake batter	*raspberry ripple ice*
8oz (225g) raspberries,	*cream for serving*
fresh or defrosted	

Scatter the raspberries with the sugar and leave them to stand for at least 30 minutes – the fruit will produce lots of delicious juice during this time.

Cook the pancakes as directed then divide the raspberries between them and roll them up. Serve the pancakes with the juice spooned over and a dollop of ice cream.

PEAR AND CINNAMON PANCAKES WITH CREAM

SERVES 4

1 quantity of basic	*1–2tbsp sugar, to taste*
pancake batter	*1¹/2oz (45g) walnuts,*
1oz (30g) butter	*finely chopped*
¹/2tsp ground cinnamon	*whipped cream to serve*
4 ripe pears, fresh or	
canned, peeled	

Prepare the filling. Heat the butter in a small pan with the cinnamon, then add the chopped pears and the sugar and cook briefly until the pears are soft and well coated with the cinnamon butter. Add the chopped nuts and keep the filling warm.

Cook the pancakes as directed, then spoon a little of the filling into each one. Spoon the juices over the pancakes and serve them with whipped cream.

MANDARIN AND SULTANA PANCAKES

SERVES 4

1 quantity of basic	*2–3tbsp clear honey*
pancake batter	*ground nutmeg*
10oz (280g) can	*ice cream or cream to*
mandarin segments	*serve*
2oz (60g) sultanas	

Prepare the filling by mixing the mandarins with the sultanas in a pan. Heat gently for 6–8 minutes, until the sultanas have swollen in the fruit juice and the juice has slightly reduced. Add the honey and nutmeg to taste and keep the filling warm.

Cook the pancakes as directed, then spoon a little of the filling into each one. Roll or fold the pancakes around the filling.

Spoon the juices over the pancakes then serve them with ice cream or cream.

SUPPER AT MILL COTTAGE

Marriage to Christopher Tate was a big change for Kathy. Her first husband, Jackie Merrick, a farmer, had been killed in a shooting accident, and she'd resisted Christopher's advances for some time, thinking they were inappropriate. When she finally accepted his proposal of marriage she became worried; life with Jackie had been simple, and they had led uncluttered lives.

In contrast, Christopher's lifestyle was one of sophistication and wealth. She asked me for advice on what I thought would be suitable to serve up at a dinner party she was organising. I offered some sug-

gestions, but in the end Kathy had her own ideas about what she felt was needed – she had already consulted glossy magazines and cookery books – she had flair, and all she lacked was expertise. As for the sophistication of the Tates' world, Kathy had nothing to fear; on an evening, when they were first married, Christopher liked nothing better than returning home from work and sitting down to a night in with his wife. He'd enjoyed late nights out on the town, with dinner in fancy restaurants, before he met Kathy – but all that changed overnight. Read on and savour Kathy's recipes, and you'll understand why!

KATHY'S EGG-FRIED RICE

SERVES 2

Kathy and Chris both enjoy Chinese food – the fact that it is quick to prepare and relatively low in fat are added bonuses.

6oz (175g) easy-cook long-grain rice	1tbsp oil
12fl oz (340ml) water (approx)	2 spring onions, finely chopped
pinch of salt	2 eggs, size 3, beaten
2oz (60g) frozen peas	2tbsp soy sauce

Measure the rice in a cup or convenient container, then place it in a saucepan with two measures of cold water – this is the easiest way to get the correct proportions of rice and water. Add a pinch of salt and bring to the boil, then stir. Cover with a lid and simmer slowly for 10 minutes. Stir in the peas, cook for a further 5 minutes then remove the pan from the heat and leave covered for 5 minutes.

Heat the oil in a large frying-pan and cook the spring onions until soft, then add the eggs and cook slowly until starting to thicken. Add the rice and stir-fry together with the soy sauce until hot. Serve immediately.

Use any leftover rice for salad.

SMOKY PEPPERED PASTA

SERVES 2

Chris and Kathy don't eat huge quantities of meat at every meal. This is one of their favourite supper dishes and the pasta makes the smoked sausage go a long way. Any leftovers reheat well for lunch. Kathy uses paprika and poppy seeds to flavour the dish instead of the more predictable herbs, which give a middle-European feel and flavour.

2tbsp olive oil	sausage with garlic, sliced
1 onion, finely chopped	7oz (200g) can chopped tomatoes
1 stick celery, finely sliced	salt and freshly ground black pepper
1 green pepper, seeded and chopped	6oz (175g) pasta
½tsp paprika	1tbsp poppy seeds
4oz (120g) smoked pork	

Cook the onion in the oil until starting to soften, then add the celery and pepper and continue cooking for 2–3 minutes. Meanwhile, bring a large pan of salted water to the boil for the pasta.

Stir the sausage and paprika into the vegetables and cook for 1–2 minutes then add the tomatoes, season and simmer for 20 minutes.

Add the pasta to the boiling water then simmer for 12 minutes or as directed on the packet – it should be tender but still have a slight bite to it when cooked.

Drain the pasta then add it to the tomato sauce, tossing it through the sauce until it is evenly coated. Season the pasta to taste then serve immediately.

CANTONESE TROUT

SERVES 2

The young Tates have easy access to trout from Home Farm and enjoy cooking it oriental-style.

*2 large trout fillets,
  weighing about 12oz
  (340g) each*
*2tbsp sunflower or
  sesame oil*
*3–4 spring onions,
  trimmed and finely
  chopped*
*1 green chilli, seeded and
  finely chopped*
*1 small piece fresh root
  ginger, peeled and
  finely sliced*

*1 clove of garlic, finely
  sliced*
*15oz (425g) can baby
  sweetcorn, drained
  and cut in half*
3tbsp hoi-sin sauce
3tbsp water
*1tbsp freshly chopped
  coriander or 1tsp
  dried*
*soy or chilli sauce for
  serving*

Skin the trout fillets, removing as many bones as possible, then cut them into 1in (2.5cm) pieces. Heat the oil in a frying-pan and cook the fish for 2–3 minutes, turning the pieces over once. Remove the trout to a plate. Add the spring onion, chilli, ginger and garlic and stir-fry until the onions are just starting to soften, then add the baby sweetcorn and cook for a further 2–3 minutes. Add the hoi-sin sauce and water

to the pan, stir to blend, then return the trout to the pan and heat for 1–2 minutes, until hot. Sprinkle with the chopped coriander, then serve immediately with soy or chilli sauce to taste.

TURKEY STIR-FRY
with Creamy Mustard Sauce

SERVES 2

Prepared turkey strips to stir-fry make a quick and economical supper dish for Kathy and Chris. Button mushrooms and crème fraîche add a touch of luxury to an affordable meal.

2tbsp olive oil
1 onion, finely chopped
*8oz (225g) turkey
  breast, cut into thin
  strips for stir-fry*
*4oz (120g) button
  mushrooms*

*2tsp smooth Dijon
  mustard*
2tbsp crème fraîche
*salt and freshly ground
  black pepper*
*freshly chopped chives
  for garnish*

Slowly cook the onion in the oil until soft but not brown, then add the turkey and stir-fry over a higher heat for 5–6 minutes, until slightly browned and just cooked. Add the mushrooms and cook for a further 2–3 minutes.

Mix the mustard and crème fraîche together then pour them into the pan. Simmer gently for a few minutes then season with salt and pepper before serving. Garnish with snipped chives if wished.

ZOE COMES TO LUNCH

Some of the recipes suggested by Christopher and Kathy were popular with the couple because they take the minimum amount of time to prepare and cook. Some time ago, Kathy decided to work with Christopher when he was running Tate's Haulage Company. He was working long hours, and it seemed as though the couple weren't seeing enough of each other, so Kathy decided to share an office with her husband. At lunchtime, she made use of the cooker in the small office kitchen, and soon they'd built up quite a variety of quick tasty snacks.

Zoe often used to call in on her brother – to see how he was – but the fact that her visits tended to coincide with lunchtime suggests she had ulterior motives! She still never refuses a bite to eat, and leaves soon after her plate has been cleared!

Now that Christopher works from home and has to grab lunch in between meetings, sessions on the word processor and long phone calls, these recipes are invaluable to him. He can organise his time, revel in his independence and still take time out to cook an enjoyable meal.

MILLSTREAM SOUP

SERVES 2–3

As he works from home, Chris often needs a quick and easy lunch which he can eat at his computer. A substantial soup with a spicy cheese scone is just right.

2tbsp olive oil	1¹/2pt (850ml) vegetable
1 large onion, finely	stock
chopped	salt and black pepper
1 large potato of about	2¹/2oz (75g) packet
12oz (340g), peeled	watercress
and diced	freshly grated nutmeg

Cook the onion in the olive oil until soft, then add the potato and stock. Bring to the boil and simmer, covered, for 15–20 minutes, until the potato is tender, then add the watercress and cook for a further 2 minutes, until it has wilted.

Cool the soup slightly then pour it into a liquidiser or food processor and blend until smooth. Rinse the pan then return the soup to it and reheat gently, seasoning and adding nutmeg to taste.

CHEESE SCONE ROUND

SERVES 2–4

An ideal accompaniment to Millstream Soup, this is quickly mixed and baked. All scones are best on the day they are made, so Kathy and Chris make only a small round which they can eat at one sitting.

4oz (120g) self-raising	1¹/2oz (45g) Cheddar
wholewheat flour	cheese, finely grated
pinch of salt	2fl oz (60ml) milk,
good pinch of paprika	approx
1oz (30g) butter	

Preheat the oven to 220°C/425°F/Gas 7 and lightly flour a baking sheet.

Mix the flour, salt and paprika together and rub in the butter then stir in the cheese. Mix to a slightly soft dough with milk and then knead the dough lightly on a floured surface until smooth. Press into a round about 3/4in (2cm) thick and place on the baking sheet, then score into 4.

Bake in the preheated oven for 15–20 minutes, then cool slightly on a wire rack before eating warm.

PERFECT POLENTA

SERVES 2

This is wonderful comfort food – very quick to prepare, and the answer to a depressing morning on the 'phone and computer. Serve with a simple salad. Use a blue cheese with plenty of bite for the topping – Gorgonzola, Stilton or Danish blue.

16fl oz (460ml) water	¹/2oz (15g) butter
4oz (120g) instant	1¹/2–2oz (45–60g) blue
polenta	cheese, preferably
salt and freshly ground	Gorgonzola
black pepper	

Bring the water to the boil in a saucepan then shoot in the rest of the ingredients except the cheese. Bring to the boil, stirring all the time – the polenta will thicken into a very stiff paste. It is important to season it whilst thickening otherwise it is difficult to distribute the seasoning evenly.

Cook the polenta over a low heat for 5 minutes or so, until the grains have softened and become fluffy. Stir the mixture frequently. Transfer to two individual ovenproof dishes and top with the cheese, which should be crumbled or sliced.

Cook the polenta under a very hot grill until the cheese has melted and is beginning to brown. Serve immediately.

ITALIAN TOAST

SERVES 2

This simple but delicious snack benefits from the tomatoes being marinaded for 30 minutes or so before they are cooked. It's the style of cooking that is Italian, not the tomatoes, although plum tomatoes do work very well in this recipe.

4 ripe tomatoes, sliced
1 clove garlic, thinly sliced
salt and freshly ground
  black pepper
2–3 leaves fresh basil,
  torn into small pieces

3–4tbsp fruity olive oil
2 slices bread
5oz (150g) mozzarella,
  thinly sliced

Place the tomatoes in a bowl with the garlic and seasonings then add the olive oil and leave for at least 30 minutes. Toast the bread under the grill on one side only. Turn it and pile the tomatoes onto the second side. Grill quickly under a very high heat until the tomatoes are just starting to blacken – make certain that they are completely covering the toast or it will burn under the fierce heat.

Lay the mozzarella slices over the tomatoes then grill again until the cheese is just starting to melt. Spoon any remaining olive oil from the marinade, or a little extra, over the tomatoes before serving.

CHRIS AND KATHY ENTERTAIN

Like most married couples, Kathy and Christopher have had their share of rough patches. They've fallen out with one another, patched things up and then fallen out again more times than I can count. Things seem pretty bad at the moment – who knows where it will all end?

Not long ago, Christopher's business folded and the comfortable lifestyle he'd enjoyed came to a temporary end. Extravagant lunches in expensive restaurants paid for by the business became a thing of the past. To cheer him up, Kathy secretly called

the managers of one or two of Christopher's favourite restaurants and begged them for the recipes of some of their tastiest dishes. No restaurateur is willing to give away the best-kept secrets of their trade, so it is credit to Kathy and her charming ways that she was able to prise several recipes from them, and prepare them over several weeks for her husband. Christopher was delighted. Kathy found herself adept at several Thai and Chinese dishes – so much so that when Chris regained his fortune, he preferred to bring clients home with him than eat out.

PISSALADIERE

SERVES 4

This isn't a complicated recipe or an expensive one – it just takes a long time to prepare properly, making it a weekends-only dish for Kathy and Chris, as for many other working couples. This makes a wonderful supper dish, an excellent starter or a good accompaniment to roast beef.

FOR THE TOPPING

1¹/2lb (680g) onions	salt and freshly ground
3tbsp olive oil	black pepper
4 small cloves garlic,	2 sprigs fresh thyme
peeled but left whole	1 bay leaf

FOR THE BASE

12oz (340g) strong	6fl oz (175ml) onion
plain flour	liquid
¹/2tsp salt	2oz (50g) can anchovy
1 sachet easy-blend yeast	fillets
2tbsp olive oil	black olives

Prepare the topping. Slice the onions finely – as there are so many of them this is least painful if done in a food processor with the slicing plate. Cook the onions in the oil in a frying-pan that has a lid until they are starting to soften, then add the garlic and seasonings. Cover the pan and cook the onions slowly for 1¹/2–2 hours, until they are very soft and caramelised – they should go brown. If the onions are still white after an hour, remove the lid from the'-

pan but continue to cook them slowly as you don't want the liquid to boil away. Strain the onions through a sieve and reserve the liquid.

Make the bread for the base. Mix the flour and salt together with the yeast then make a well in the centre and add the olive oil. Make up the onion liquid to 6fl oz (175ml) with water if necessary, then add it to the bowl. Mix to a manageable dough and knead thoroughly for about 10 minutes, until smooth and elastic. Roll and stretch the dough then place it in a shallow tin about 8x12in (20x30cm). Cover and leave in a warm place for 30 minutes, or until well risen.

Preheat the oven to 220°C/425°F/Gas 7. Top the dough with the onion mixture, removing the thyme and bay leaves. Arrange the anchovy fillets over the onion then garnish with as many olives as you like. Top with a little extra black pepper then bake the pissaladière in the preheated oven for 25–30 minutes. Serve with a side salad.

THAI GREEN CHICKEN CURRY

SERVES 2

Kathy and Chris like to experiment in the kitchen and the weekend is the time for trying out some unusual dishes, when there is the time to search out exotic seasonings and ingredients. The Thai spices used in this recipe can be bought fresh in packets in most large supermarkets, and the fish sauce and coconut milk will also be available there.

FOR THE CURRY PASTE

1 large green pepper, seeded and diced	*1tsp ground coriander*
2 green chillis, seeded and finely sliced	*1 piece lemon grass, outer skin removed and flesh finely chopped*
1 small piece fresh root ginger, peeled and finely chopped	*2tbsp fish sauce*
2 medium onions, chopped	*5 fresh lime leaves or 2tbsp freshly chopped coriander*

FOR THE CURRY

2tbsp groundnut oil	*2tbsp freshly chopped coriander leaves*
2 chicken breasts, skinned and diced	*3–4 fresh basil leaves, shredded*
1 small aubergine, sliced	*1tbsp granulated sugar*
8fl oz (225ml) thick coconut milk	*salt to taste*
1 small green pepper, seeded and sliced	*1 large fresh lime leaf, shredded*
1tbsp fish sauce	

Place all the ingredients for the curry paste in a liquidiser or food processor and blend until thick and almost smooth.

Heat the oil in a frying-pan, add the curry paste and cook for about 5 minutes – add a little of the coconut milk if necessary. Add the chicken breast and stir-fry for 3–4 minutes before adding the aubergine and coconut milk. Stir in the green pepper and all the remaining ingredients except the lime leaf. Bring to the boil then simmer slowly for 20–25 minutes, until the chicken is tender, adding a little water if necessary. Check the seasoning then stir in the lime leaf. Serve with rice or noodles.

LEMON MERINGUE ICE CREAM

SERVES 4–6

An excellent dinner-party dish and one that can be prepared well in advance. It is also an indulgent dessert for dipping into whenever the fancy takes you – which it will.

FOR THE MERINGUE

1 egg white, size 2	*2oz (60g) caster sugar*

FOR THE LEMON FILLING

1 lemon, grated rind and juice	*3fl oz (90ml) water*
1tbsp (heaped) cornflour	*2oz (60g) caster sugar*
	1 egg yolk, size 2

FOR THE ICE CREAM

2 egg whites, size 2	*1/4pt (150ml) thick natural yogurt*
5oz (150g) caster sugar	*1/2pt (280ml) whipping cream*
6tbsp water	

Preheat the oven to 160°C/325°F/Gas 3. Whisk the egg white for the meringue until stiff, then gradually whisk in the sugar. Spread the mixture (1in [2.5cm] thick) onto silicone paper on a baking sheet. Bake in the preheated oven for about 45 minutes, until pale golden and crisp. Allow to cool, then break into pieces.

Prepare the lemon filling by mixing the lemon rind, juice and cornflour to a smooth paste. Add this to the water in a small pan and bring to the boil, whisking constantly. Remove the pan from the heat, shoot in the sugar and whisk until it has dissolved Allow to cool slightly before whisking in the egg yolk. Spread the mixture out on a piece of silicone paper and allow it to cool completely before chopping roughly.

Prepare the ice cream when the meringue and the lemon mixture have cooled. Whisk the egg whites until stiff whilst dissolving the sugar in the water. Bring the sugar mixture to the boil then boil it for 3 minutes. Gradually pour the thickened syrup onto the egg whites, whisking constantly, continue whisking whilst cooling. Add the yogurt and whisk until the mixture is completely cool.

Whip the cream until thickened but not stiff, then fold it into the yogurt. Fold the meringue and the lemon into the ice cream then transfer it to a loaf tin, bombe tin or freezer container. Freeze for at least 4 hours and remove from the freezer 20 minutes before serving. It does not require whisking whilst freezing.

GINGER AND PISTACHIO CREAM

SERVES 4

This rich and creamy dessert should be eaten only in small amounts – it is wonderful!

9oz (250g) mascarpone cheese	*4tbsp syrup from ginger*
4 pieces stem ginger, finely chopped	*1 1/2oz (45g) pistachio kernels, roughly chopped*

Beat the mascarpone until smooth then add the ginger and syrup and mix well before stirring in the pistachios. Keep beating after adding the syrup – the mascarpone will become smooth again. Add a little sugar if necessary, then pile into individual glasses. Chill, and serve with fresh fruit or with brandy snaps.

SETH'S ONE-POT MEALS

I was very concerned to hear that Seth had decided against setting up house with Betty Eagleton late last year. I made it known to him that I thought he was a fool to choose solitary life in a caravan rather than a warm house with a woman who adored him. He told me that he was a bit too long in the teeth to be taking advice from a pub landlord. I reminded him that he didn't have any teeth.

It turned out I was wrong…Seth found a new lease of life living in that small caravan. He always did enjoy a frugal existence, even when he was married to Meg. He has changed though – it suddenly struck me one evening in The Woolpack that I hadn't seen him ordering food for a while. I put it down to the fact that Betty must be feeding him. Quite the con-trary – Seth was cooking for himself. He found a saucepan and an old pot in an outhouse up at Emmerdale Farm one day; the Sugdens didn't want them so he took them home, and he hasn't looked back since. Betty confirmed that he'd become quite a gourmet…I found this rather difficult to believe. Still, whatever my opinion, there can be no denying the fact that Seth has provided me with some delicious recipes – real poacher's food – warm and filling. Seth might not have central heating, but with the food he eats, he barely needs it!

POACHER'S BROTH

SERVES 3–4

A rabbit cooks into a satisfying and tasty broth, especially when sweet parsnips and pearl barley are added. Pan-fry the saddle of the rabbit separately if you wish – it is a bit wasted in a soup.

2tbsp oil	2 medium parsnips,
1 large onion	peeled and diced
1 rabbit, skinned and	2oz (60g) pearl barley
jointed or 12oz (340g)	2pt (1.14l) vegetable or
boneless rabbit, diced	chicken stock
flour	salt and freshly ground
1tsp curry powder	black pepper

Heat the oil in a large pan and cook the onion until soft. Lightly dredge the rabbit with flour, then add it to the pan with the curry powder and brown. Stir in the parsnips and pearl barley, then add the stock and seasonings and bring to the boil. Cover and simmer for at least 1 hour, until the rabbit is tender.

Take the meat from the bone, dice the rabbit and return it to the pan. Reheat the broth if necessary, then season to taste and serve.

PORKY PIGEON PUDDING

SERVES 3–4

Pigeon breasts can be a little dry so cooking them with sausagemeat in a suet pudding is a good way to keep them moist and succulent.

8oz (225g) self-raising	1lb (460g) pork
flour	sausagemeat
salt and freshly ground	1 small onion, very
black pepper	finely chopped
4oz (120g) shredded suet	4 pigeon breasts

Prepare the suet pastry. Mix the flour with a pinch of salt in a bowl, stir in the suet then mix to a soft manageable dough with cold water. Turn onto a floured surface and knead lightly. Roll out two thirds of the pastry and use it to line a 1½pt (850ml) pudding basin.

Mix the sausagemeat with the onion and a little salt and pepper. Place half the mixture in the lined pudding basin, then cover with the pigeon breasts and top with the remaining sausagemeat.

Roll out the remaining suet pastry to cover the pudding, damping the edges to seal them together.

Cover the pudding with greased greaseproof paper and foil, tying it securely in place with string. Simmer the pudding for 2 hours.

BETTY'S PAN-FRIED TICKLED TROUT

SERVES 1

You don't have to be a gourmet to recognise that the flavour of a freshly caught brown trout is delicious – a countryman like Seth knows that he is in for a treat when he 'happens across' a brown trout. Rainbow trout may also be cooked in this way.

1 brown trout, cleaned	salt and freshly ground
1 rasher smoked streaky	black pepper
bacon, rinded	1oz (30g) butter

Trim the trout and cut off the head and tail if it is too large to fit into your frying-pan. Stretch the bacon with the back of a knife and then wrap it around the fish; season lightly.

Melt the butter in a frying-pan, add the trout and fry quickly for about 5 minutes on each side. Serve the trout with the browned butter poured over it.

JOCK McDONALD'S SOUP

SERVES 2–3

This rich brew is really more of a stew than a soup – it is based on an old Scottish recipe given to Seth by the infamous Jock McDonald. Use the saddle meat in a stir-fry rather than adding it to the soup, if preferred.

1 young hare, skinned	salt and freshly ground
and jointed	black pepper
2 onions, finely sliced	2½pt (1.4l) stock, or to
2 carrots, finely sliced	cover
2 turnips, chopped	1oz (30g) fine or
6 peppercorns	medium oatmeal
2tbsp freshly chopped	freshly chopped parsley
mixed herbs	to garnish

Place the hare, vegetables, seasonings and stock in a large pan and bring to the boil. Simmer, covered, for about 2½ hours, until the hare is tender. Add a little more stock during cooking if necessary.

Strain the soup through a large sieve. Dice the hare meat finely, then discard the bones and the vegetables. Return the meat to the pan with the stock and add the oatmeal. Bring to the boil and simmer for 5 minutes, then season to taste with salt and pepper – it may be necessary to add a little more stock if the soup has reduced dramatically.

Garnish with freshly chopped parsley and serve.

AUTUMN HARVEST

Seth will only buy groceries from the Windsors' shop when he's forced to. Most of the time he's at his happiest picking mushrooms from the fields at the crack of dawn, or rooting around under hedgerows for edible plants and herbs. Once he even borrowed a pig to go truffle hunting. Thankfully, his plans to go into business supplying truffles to the restaurant trade came to nothing when the pig ran amok in the village and upset a lot of people – me included!

The wonderful thing about Seth is that he remembers age-old recipes which most of us haven't even heard of. Fifty years ago, and more, farming folk thought nothing of sitting down to a bowl of nettle soup, or drinking a glass of elderberry wine. But the recipes have been lost and their ingredients forgotten. Only Seth seems aware that the hedgerows, rivers and forests offer a wide supply of foodstuffs that you and I wouldn't even think about.

PHEASANT POT

SERVES 2

A more pretentious cook than Seth might call this dish 'Pot roasted pheasant with glazed root vegetables'. To Seth it is a simple stew to cook in the caravan in one pot, using a young pheasant and freshly dug root vegetables from his allotment. Cut the pheasant into portions before cooking if wished – Seth usually cooks the bird whole and then takes the meat off the bone.

1 onion	*salt and freshly ground*
2 large carrots	*black pepper*
1 medium parsnip	*2 bay leaves*
1 large turnip	*1/2pt (280ml) stock*
2 sticks celery	*freshly chopped parsley*
1oz (30g) butter	*to garnish*
1 pheasant	

Cut the prepared vegetables into large 2in (5cm) chunks. Melt the butter in a deep pan that will just fit the bird and brown the pheasant on all sides, then remove it and add the vegetables. Brown them quickly on all sides in the butter, then remove them too.

Return the pheasant to the pan, season lightly and add the bay leaves, then place the vegetables on top of the bird. Pour in the stock, cover the pan and simmer slowly for 1 hour, or until the pheasant is cooked through.

Serve the pheasant in portions with the vegetables. Boil the stock to reduce it slightly to make an accompanying sauce, and garnish the dish with freshly chopped parsley.

AUTUMN FRUITS
with Cinnamon Dumplings

SERVES 2

This delicious dessert is simple to make and very cheap when the Bramleys are ready on the trees and blackberries and elderberries are ripe in the hedgerows.

2 large cooking apples,	*2oz (60g) self-raising*
peeled and sliced	*flour*
8oz (225g) hedgerow	*1oz (30g) shredded suet*
fruits	*good pinch of cinnamon*
1/4pt (150ml) water	*1tsp sugar*
sugar to taste	

Place the apples and berries in a saucepan with the water and cook until just starting to soften. Add sugar to taste. Mix the flour, suet, cinnamon and remaining sugar in a bowl and add water to make a soft but manageable dough. Knead lightly, then shape into small dumplings.

Drop the dumplings into the pan of simmering fruit, cover and cook for about 15 minutes. Scatter extra sugar over the fruit and dumplings just before serving.

ELDERBERRY QUENCHER

MAKES ABOUT 1PT (570ML)

Elderflowers make a cordial which turns into a delicious 'champagne'-style drink when diluted with sparkling mineral water. Seth always seems to be too busy in the early summer with his allotment to gather the flowers so he waits until late summer to harvest the berries to make his cordial. Always try to gather the berries away from the roadside, where they will not have been subjected to too many traffic fumes.

1lb (460g) heads ripe	*pinch of ground allspice*
elderberries – about 2	*1lb (460g) granulated*
carrier bags full	*sugar*
1 1/2pt (680ml) water	

Wash the elderberries thoroughly in plenty of water and remove the stalks from the heads, leaving only the clusters of berries on their thin stalks. Transfer them to a large pan and add the water and allspice. Bring to the boil then simmer the fruits for about 30 minutes, until they have all softened and burst.

Strain the juice through a sieve lined with muslin and return it to the pan. Add the sugar and boil until reduced to a slightly syrupy liquid – taste the liquid as it comes to the boil to check the sweetness; the cordial should be slightly sharp.

Cool the cordial, then transfer it to a sealed container and store it in the refrigerator. Dilute with water or mineral water before drinking.

Seth has always been a law unto himself – he's unique. They broke the mould when they made him. One day, when the two of us are in our dotage, I intend to sit him down and make him write out his rules and regulations of the countryside, and his code of practice for the seasons. If civilisation came to an end, and the human race was forced to fend for itself, Seth would survive and thrive; he knows the right places to look for food, the correct berries to eat, the safest water to drink. He learned all this from his father, who learned it from *his* father, and Seth hasn't passed on that knowledge to anyone else, as far as I'm aware. I'm grateful to him for his contributions; they might look rather straightforward to some, but I think they're unique. Just remember, when you're preparing his recipes in the safety and comfort of your kitchen, that Seth is probably out there in the wild stalking his prey, tickling trout, gathering herbs... there's a lot to be said for the convenience of the local supermarket!

SETH'S SINFUL TIPPLE

A bottle of gin is a considerable expense, but well worth it for the large amount of delicious liqueur that this recipe produces. Damsons produce a wonderful drink if you can find them – if not, flavour your gin with sloes. This produces a strongly flavoured, sweet and potent drink to be consumed only in sherry glass quantities.

2lb (900g) damsons or sloes	*2lb (900g) granulated sugar*
	1³/4pt (1l) gin

Wash the fruit and prick them all over with a fork. Place them in a large china or glass bowl with the sugar, add the gin and stir well. Cover with a lid or tray (plastic wrap may allow some of the alcohol to escape!) and stir once a day for a month.

Strain the flavoured gin to remove the fruit and bottle the liquid. Make this liqueur when the damsons or sloes are ripe and it will be ready for Christmas. (If using damsons, the fruit makes a quite exceptional crumble after being removed from the gin!)

SETH'S ALLOTMENT

When I opened The Woolpack wine bar, I had the romantic notion that it would generate employment in the village. With this in mind I decided to use local produce; the meat would be supplied by nearby farmers, and the fruit and vegetables, where possible, would come from local growers. I knew Seth had an allotment, so when he told me he was interested in supplying my vegetable needs, I asked to look at his produce. He brought me some exquisite examples, and as a result got the contract.

What he failed to tell me was that I was the owner of the allotment – it belonged to The Woolpack! Seth was selling my own vegetables to me. Once we'd sorted out the minor problem of ownership, Seth took over the allotment. He definitely has green fingers; his vegetables – notably his marrows – have won prizes and acclaim throughout the Dales. The recipes he's suggested here make good use of country vegetables, but you don't have to have your own allotment or garden to appreciate them.

BETTY'S BRAISED CELERY WITH TOMATOES

SERVES 2

It's not easy to grow a good head of blanched celery, but Seth's many years on the allotment have taught him a thing or two about trenching and irrigation. He says all the work is worthwhile as blanched celery has a better flavour than green varieties.

2tbsp oil	*14oz (400g) can*
1 onion, finely chopped	*chopped tomatoes with*
4 rashers streaky bacon,	*herbs or fennel*
chopped	*1 small head celery*
salt and freshly ground	
black pepper	

Cook the onion and bacon slowly in the oil until the onion is softened but not browned. Add the tomatoes with a little seasoning and bring to the boil.

Trim the celery and chop it into 1in (2.5cm) pieces – leave any leaves on the heart as they will add colour and flavour to the finished dish. Scatter the celery over the tomato base, cover the pan and reduce the heat. Simmer the celery slowly for 30 minutes, or until just tender. Serve the celery with the tomato sauce spooned over it.

SUMMER VEGETABLE SALAD

SERVES 2

By the time Seth's French beans and mangetout are ready on the allotment, the asparagus is well established and less of a treat. Seth gathers what vegetables are ready and just blanches them in the morning. By lunchtime or in the evening they combine with a light dressing to make a delicious salad.

8oz (225g) asparagus,	*8oz (225g) French*
trimmed	*beans, trimmed*
8oz (225g) mangetout,	*6tbsp garlic-flavoured*
trimmed	*vinaigrette*

Bring a large pan of salted water to the boil. Cut the asparagus spears in half and add the stalk ends to the pan. Simmer for 5 minutes, then add the spears and cook for a further 3 minutes. Stir in the mangetout and beans and simmer for a further 3 minutes. Be certain to return the vegetables to the boil each time more are added to the pan. Drain the vegetables and plunge them immediately into a bowl of cold water – leave until they are quite cold.

Drain the vegetables and chill lightly in the 'fridge for 30 minutes. Toss in the vinaigrette and serve.

SPRING BEANS

SERVES 4

The only trouble with broad beans is that their season is so short! This recipe works well with freshly picked beans, or with frozen ones. The spring onion sauce accentuates the spring freshness of this popular vegetable. The sauce is purposely thin, so that it coats the beans but doesn't drown them.

1lb (460g) broad beans,	*1oz (30g) flour*
shelled weight	*3/4pt (430ml) milk*
1oz (30g) butter	*salt and freshly ground*
1 bunch spring onions,	*black pepper*
finely chopped	

Cook the broad beans in boiling salted water for about 10 minutes, until just tender. Drain and set to one side.

Melt the butter in a pan, add the spring onions and cook slowly until soft but not browned. Stir in the flour and cook for a few seconds, then remove the pan from the heat. Gradually beat in the milk.

Bring the sauce to the boil over a medium heat, stirring continually. Season the sauce then add the drained beans, and continue to cook for 2–3 minutes before serving.

SETH'S WACKY COLESLAW

SERVES 2–3

This salad is a complete meal in itself – the Frankfurters and pickled cucumbers give it a Germanic flavour and make it more filling than ordinary coleslaw. Quantities of vegetables can be varied according to taste. Serve this salad with fresh, crusty bread.

8oz (225g) crisp white or green cabbage, shredded
1 small onion, very finely sliced
2 carrots, coarsely grated
4 small Frankfurters
2 sweet and sour cucumbers or gherkins, sliced
salt and freshly ground black pepper
5–6tbsp mayonnaise

Mix all the prepared vegetables together then add the sliced Frankfurters and cucumbers. Season then bind the salad together with mayonnaise.

FIELD FARE SALAD

SERVES 2

Dandelion leaves make a wonderful salad, but they must be picked young. The leaves are at their best in the spring. Seth combines the leaves with young beetroots from his allotment to make a simple salad.

4oz (120g) dandelion leaves
4 small beetroots, freshly
cooked and peeled
3tbsp vinaigrette
freshly chopped chives

Wash the leaves and tear out the middle stalks, as you would prepare spinach. Arrange the leaves on a plate and then top them with the beetroots, thinly sliced. Spoon the vinaigrette over the salad and then garnish with chopped chives before serving.

MALLOW SOUP

SERVES 2

The common mallow is, as its name suggests, plentiful in the countryside. It keeps its leaves virtually all year but the pink flowers are only in bloom in the summer. The best time to pick the leaves is when the plant is in bloom – which also aids recognition. Pick the leaves without any stalk.

2oz (60g) common mallow leaves
1oz (30g) butter
1 clove garlic, crushed
1pt (570ml) well-flavoured stock
salt and freshly ground black pepper

Wash the leaves and shred them finely. Cook the garlic with the leaves in the butter until they are starting to wilt, then add the stock and bring to the boil. Simmer the soup for 30 minutes, then allow it to cool slightly before pouring into a liquidiser or food processor and blending until smooth.

Rinse the pan and return the soup to it. Season to taste, reheat if necessary then serve. Some people like to gather a few of the mallow flowers to serve in the soup as a garnish.

HOT STINGER

SERVES 4

Nettle soup is really a spring dish – the nettles only taste good when they are young so they have to be gathered early. Seth grows landcress on his allotment so he adds a little of that to the soup for extra flavour – you could use watercress if you prefer.

1lb (460g) young nettle tops – take care gathering them!
3tbsp oil
1 onion, finely chopped
1 small potato, peeled and diced
1½pt (680ml) well-flavoured stock
salt and freshly ground black pepper
1 handful landcress or watercress

Wash the nettles thoroughly then shake them dry and chop them roughly. Melt the butter in a large pan, add the onion and cook slowly until soft but not brown. Stir in the potato, add the stock and bring to the boil. Season lightly, then simmer the soup for 20–30 minutes, until the potato is tender. Add the landcress and continue cooking briefly until it has wilted.

Allow the soup to cool slightly, then pour it into a liquidiser or food processor and blend until smooth. Rinse the saucepan, then return the soup to it and reheat it gently, seasoning to taste. Serve with fresh rolls or crusty bread.

MEADOW TEA

When there is plenty of clover in the fields Seth gathers the white flowers to make a refreshing tisane, an infusion that is drunk like tea. It has a glorious pale green colour. To make enough for two cups pour 1pt (570ml) of boiling water over 2tbsp of white clover flowers in a jug and leave to infuse for at least 5 minutes – the longer you leave it (up to 10 minutes), the better the flavour. Strain the infusion before drinking hot or cold.

A Poacher's Tale

Seth often complains that his job is the most difficult in the village; it's mostly night work, it can be life-threatening, it's antisocial and there's little praise for a job well done. He's only joking of course, but he does have a point. To a lot of people who don't know him very well, he's the old man with the whiskers who spends most of his waking hours propped up against the bar of The Woolpack. Actually this couldn't be further from the truth – it's an image Seth has cultivated to protect himself. The unsuspecting villagers are blissfully unaware that as soon as I close my doors to customers on an evening, Seth's working day is about to begin. He's off into the woods in search of rabbit, trout and pheasant.

I'm quite comfortable with Seth's profession now, but it was different in the old days. I was the landowner convinced Seth was robbing me, but I could never prove it. For years he was the scourge of the Verneys, the family who owned Home Farm and the surrounding land. Squire Verney failed to put a stop to his activities and so did I. The landowners and farmers of Emmerdale breathed a sigh of relief when Seth went 'legit'. He became a gamekeeper. In fact he became my gamekeeper; the thought being, what better way to stop poaching than to employ the best poacher in the area! I've always felt he made a better poacher than a gamekeeper though. His dinner hour seemed to last most of the afternoon and I never knew from one moment to the next where he was. I actually spent an afternoon following him once. The wicked man knew I was behind him and he led me into the muddiest field I've ever seen in my life. At least my game birds were in good hands. If nothing else he was trustworthy; on two occasions he was injured protecting my birds from poachers.

The saying 'You can't teach an old dog new tricks' springs to mind because ultimately Seth returned to his old poaching ways. He lost his job as Frank Tate's gamekeeper and a man has to learn a living somehow. Seth had no choice. But Seth is also a man who needs a certain amount of excitement and mischief in his life and gamekeeping never really satisfied him. He's happier now. Stealing Frank Tate's pheasants and selling them in the post office is just one example of the man's deviousness. Finding and shooting the Beast of Beckindale demonstrates his excellent stalking abilities. On a serious note, Seth was able to put his poaching talents to good use when he traced the whereabouts of those evil post office raiders. He was more than a match for any sniffer dog. He was a true hero that day and my respect for his talents is immense. The man grows older but his outlook on life remains youthful. I sometimes envy his simple life.

EASTER FAIR

Frank Tate is a feared figure to many people in the community. They dislike his plans for the future, and object to what he's doing to the countryside with his leisure interests and his new-fangled farming practices. To some extent they're right in that Frank is striving for change in the countryside, but he's also a traditionalist at heart. He wants to see a renaissance of country life – and that's one of the reasons why he allowed the Easter Fair to take place at the Holiday Village. It shows off all the things that are good about the countryside. Easter bonnet and egg-rolling competitions are the highlights of the fair, but it's also a time when local craft traders and cottage industries can show off their wares.

Ned and Jan Glover's friends, the Sedgewicks (former farmers) set up their ice-cream stand and take orders for the rest of the year. Robert Sugden likes to enter the 'Paint an Easter Egg' competition, Biff tried to win it for him last year by painting the egg for Robert while the adjudicator had his back turned. Sadly, Biff's drawing abilities weren't up to much and the prize went to Alice Bates. Luke and Jessica McAllister gorge themselves on home-made sweets and biscuits. But nobody enjoys the fair more than I do! I just can't resist the Hotten Bakery stand, with its tempting cakes and mouthwatering buns.

I much prefer the Easter Fair to the Hotten Show, which takes place later in the year. There's something optimistic and jolly about Easter-time. Maybe it's the newborn lambs frolicking in the pastures, or the calves calling to their mothers; people seem more prepared to enjoy themselves at the Easter Fair. It's all about sharing and giving. Zoe Tate gives up her free time to judge the best pet competition. Dr McAllister – when he was here last – judged the Glamorous Granny competition. I tend to avoid any sort of involvement in such affairs. I was the judge who had to make the final decision when Caroline Bates and

Elizabeth Pollard were joint winners of the Glamorous Granny competition a few years ago. My deciding vote made Mrs Pollard the champion, and I wasn't very popular with Caroline for quite some time, I can tell you! To this day she won't let me forget it. There's always a tug-of-war

contest too…and that famous time when Seth tried to put a ferret down his trousers…but I digress. If Annie Sugden is around then it's an extra bonus. I buy several cakes from her stall and stick them in the freezer when I get home, but Caroline says she doesn't know why I bother as they never have time to freeze – they're eaten in such a short space of time!

When I was a child, Easter was an exciting time. We made and painted papier-mâché eggs, rolled hard-boiled eggs down a hill and ate toffee apples. The only drawback was the stiffness and formality of the occasion. All the children wore their best outfits – usually bought especially for the Easter holiday – starched shirts with ties fastened tightly, and woe betide anyone who tried to take them off. New shoes, uncomfortable due to the stiffness of the leather, made playing painful. Today, it's different – and I'd love to be a child at Easter – with so much chocolate to plough through, fairground attractions to play on endlessly, comfortable shoes on their feet. Even the Dingles appear to enjoy the Home Farm Easter Fair – their faces light up with childlike enthusiasm. At least that's what it looks like. (I know Nellie likes to taste the homemade English wines.) Even when the stalls have been emptied of their produce, the amusements and side shows put away, and the litter swept up, there's still a hint of excitement in the air; summer is only a month or two around the corner and with the summer comes warm weather, long light evenings and holidays. The Easter Fair heralds the prospect of joyful days to come.

HOT CROSS BUNS

MAKES 12

Shop-bought hot cross buns are a great disappointment when compared to homemade buns or those from a small, traditional baker.

1oz (30g) yeast
¼pt (150ml) warm milk and water, mixed
1lb (460g) strong plain flour
½tsp salt
1tsp grated nutmeg
1tsp ground mixed spice

1tsp ground cinnamon
3oz (90g) caster sugar
3oz (90g) butter
1 egg, size 3, beaten
2oz (60g) currants
2oz (60g) sultanas
2oz (60g) chopped mixed peel

FOR THE PASTE

2oz (60g) butter
4oz (120g) plain flour
8tbsp water

FOR THE GLAZE

1½oz (45g) caster sugar
3fl oz (90ml) milk and water, mixed

Crumble the yeast into the warm milk and water and leave for 3–4 minutes, then stir to dissolve the yeast completely. Mix the flour, salt, spices and sugar together in a large bowl, then rub in the butter. Add the beaten egg and the yeast liquid and mix to a soft but manageable dough – add a little extra warm water if necessary.

Turn the dough out onto a floured surface and knead it thoroughly until smooth and elastic – this will take about 10 minutes. Return the dough to the bowl and leave covered for about 1 hour, until it has doubled in size.

Scrape the dough out of the bowl onto a floured surface and knead it lightly, this is called 'knocking back'. Work in the fruit and peel, then divide the dough into 12 pieces and shape them into buns. Place on a floured baking sheet, cover and leave in a warm place for 30 minutes, until well risen.

Meanwhile, preheat the oven to 220°C/425°F/Gas 7 and prepare the paste for the crosses. Beat the butter and flour together and then work in the water to make a thick paste. Transfer the paste to a piping bag fitted with a ¼in (6mm) plain nozzle. Cut a cross in the top of each bun with a sharp knife and pipe a cross of paste over the cuts, then bake the buns in the preheated oven for 20–25 minutes.

Prepare the glaze while the buns are cooking. Heat the sugar and milk and water together over a low heat until the sugar has dissolved, then boil rapidly for about 2 minutes to make a thick syrup. Transfer the cooked buns to a wire rack and brush them immediately with the glaze. Allow the buns to cool, then serve them fresh or toasted with butter.

EMMERDALE
EASTER BISCUITS

MAKES ABOUT 20

These are the traditional spicy fruited biscuits of Easter, and are actually one of the easiest of biscuits to make, although there are always plenty for sale up at the Easter Fair.

6oz (175g) plain flour	*3oz (90g) butter*
pinch of salt	*3oz (90g) caster sugar*
1/2tsp mixed spice	*2oz (60g) currants*
1/2tsp ground cinnamon	*1 egg, size 3, beaten*

Preheat the oven to 180°C/350°F/Gas 4 and lightly grease two baking sheets. Mix the flour, salt and spices together in a bowl and rub in the butter until the mixture resembles fine breadcrumbs. Stir in the sugar and currants then make a well in the centre and add the beaten egg. Gradually mix together to form a stiff dough.

Turn the dough out onto a floured surface and knead lightly until smooth. Roll out until 1/4in (6mm) thick, then stamp out the biscuits using a 2in (5cm) cutter. Place them on the prepared baking sheets and prick them lightly with a fork.

Bake the biscuits for 12–15 minutes, until a pale golden brown. Allow them to set on the baking sheets for a few minutes, before transferring them to a wire rack to cool completely. Store in an air-tight tin.

HOMEMADE MARZIPAN

MAKES ABOUT 2LB (900G)

Because homemade marzipan is always made with ground almonds, and not with a mixture of almonds and other, cheaper nuts, it always has a superior flavour and a much paler colour. Any stall at the Easter Fair offering such marzipan is bound to sell out almost immediately.

2 eggs, size 3	*few drops of almond*
8oz (225g) caster sugar	*essence*
8oz (225g) icing sugar,	*1lb (460g) ground*
sieved	*almonds*
1tbsp dry sherry	*extra icing sugar*

Whisk the eggs and the sugars together in a bowl until thick, pale and creamy. Either do this with an electric table mixer, or in a bowl over a pan of hot water; the heat will help the eggs to thicken more quickly.

When the mixture is thick enough for you to write a word in it, remove the bowl to a cool work surface and whisk in the sherry and almond essence, then gradually fold in the ground almonds. This should produce a soft but manageable marzipan dough – if it is too wet add a little extra sieved icing sugar.

Turn the marzipan out onto a work surface covered with icing sugar and knead lightly until smooth. Use the marzipan as required, but keep it wrapped or covered until you use it to prevent a crust forming.

Use the marzipan for decorating cakes, for stuffed pitted dates, or for making marzipan fruits – all you need for these is some petit four cases to put the fruits in when they are finished, some food colourings and some patience.

EASTER FESTIVAL RING

MAKES I

This is a yeasted tea ring – it is not complicated to make and is a worthy alternative to a Simnel Cake for the centrepiece of the Easter tea table. This one is filled with marzipan and sultanas – use chopped mixed peel if you prefer. It is best eaten within 2 days of being made.

1/2oz (15g) yeast	*1 egg, size 3, beaten*
3fl oz (90ml) warm	*3tbsp sieved apricot jam*
milk	*3oz (90g) sultanas,*
8oz (225g) strong plain	*soaked for 1 hour in*
flour	*2tbsp sherry*
pinch of salt	*4oz (120g) marzipan*
2oz (60g) caster sugar	*1 egg, size 3, beaten*
3oz (90g) butter	

FOR THE ICING

4oz (120g) icing sugar,	*1oz (30g) chopped*
sieved	*toasted hazelnuts*
juice of half a lemon	

Crumble the yeast into the warm milk and leave for 3–4 minutes, then stir until the yeast is completely dissolved. Mix the flour, salt and sugar together in a large bowl, then rub in 2oz (60g) of the butter. Make a well in the centre then add the beaten egg and the yeast liquid and mix to a soft but manageable dough.

Turn out onto a lightly floured surface and knead thoroughly until smooth and elastic – this will take about 10 minutes. Return the dough to the bowl, cover and leave in a warm place for about 1 hour, until doubled in size.

Melt the remaining butter and allow it to cool slightly. Scrape the dough out onto a floured work surface and knead it lightly. Roll it out into a rectangle about 16x12in (40x30cm) and brush with the melted butter, then the apricot jam, and scatter the sultanas over the dough.

Form the marzipan into a roll and place it along one of the long sides of the dough. Roll the dough up and seal the edge with beaten egg. Shape the roll into a ring on a floured baking sheet, sealing the ends together with beaten egg. Cover and leave for a further 30–45 minutes in a warm place, until well risen.

Preheat the oven to 200°C/400°F/Gas 6. Brush the ring with the remaining beaten egg then slash the dough across the ring, from the inner to outer edges. Bake in the preheated oven for about 30 minutes, until golden brown and the underside of the dough appears cooked, then transfer to a wire rack to cool.

Mix the icing sugar with sufficient lemon juice to give a slightly runny icing, then spoon it over the tea ring, allowing it to run slowly down the sides. Scatter the chopped hazelnuts over the tea ring while the icing is still wet then allow it to set before slicing and serving.

ANNIE'S SIMNEL CAKE

MAKES 1 LARGE CAKE

Simnel cakes were originally baked for Mothering Sunday, the one day in Lent when girls in service went home to their mothers. None of the girls in Emmerdale would consider going into service now so such traditions are shunned. Simnel cakes are more often served at Easter, and should be topped with 11 small balls of marzipan to represent the 11 true disciples of Christ, Judas having been dropped after the betrayal.

1lb (460g) prepared marzipan
6oz (175g) butter
6oz (175g) caster sugar
3 eggs, size 3, beaten
8oz (225g) plain flour
pinch of salt
1lb (460g) dried mixed fruit including peel
3–4tbsp milk
3tbsp sieved apricot jam

Preheat the oven to 160°C/325°F/Gas 3 and line a 7–8in (17.5–20cm) cake tin with silicone paper. Divide the marzipan into three and keep one portion covered. Roll out the remaining pieces into one large circle the same size as the cake tin and set aside until required.

Cream the butter and sugar together until pale and fluffy then gradually beat in the eggs. Mix the flour, salt and spices together and fold them into the mixture, alternating with the fruit. Add as much milk as necessary to give a soft dropping consistency.

Spoon half the cake mixture into the prepared tin, smooth the top and cover with the marzipan, then top with the remaining cake mixture. Bake the cake in the preheated oven for 1 hour then reduce the heat to 150°C/300°F/Gas 2 and cook for a further 2–3 hours, until a skewer inserted into the centre of the cake comes out clean. The cake is cooked at a very low temperature to stop the marzipan becoming chewy.

Allow the cake to cool slightly in the tin before turning out to cool on a wire rack. Form the remaining marzipan into 11 small balls. When the cake is cold, brush the top with sieved apricot jam then arrange the marzipan balls on top of the cake. Brush them with the glaze then flash cook the top of the cake under a very hot grill, to just brown the tops of the marzipan balls – don't leave it for too long or they will melt. Allow to cool again before serving.

RACHEL AT JOE'S COTTAGE

Rachel was an enthusiastic carnivore until she moved to Emmerdale Farm with her mother, Kate, and brother Mark, to live with Joe. It was the first time she'd ever been on a farm; before that she had a romantic notion of what farm life was all about. It was quite an eye-opener for her! She fell in love with the calves and the newborn lambs, and then decided that she could no longer eat meat. It caused quite a stir in the Sugden household. Annie was offended – she thought Rachel didn't like her cooking. Joe thought she was being ridiculous, and her mother was plain embarrassed. Rachel stuck to her principles and to this day hasn't wavered from her stance. Annie rose to the challenge and kept a sharp lookout for tasty vegetarian dishes for her new granddaughter. She soon built up an impressive collection, and the recipes given here are just a small selection from Rachel's extensive repertoire.

Rachel has always had an independent streak; from an early age she was headstrong and always determined to do her own thing, so when she decided to go to Leeds University to study English Literature Joe, her stepfather, knew she'd be able to cope. Whenever she came back – which was frequently – Annie always made sure she returned with armfuls of home-cooked food. But in fact Rachel was always a great cook and she didn't really need Annie's home-baked handouts!

I think Rachel eventually regretted moving away from the village, and she began spending more time in Emmerdale than in Leeds. I even gave her a weekend job at The Woolpack – she was a regular visitor. Moving into Joe's cottage seemed a sensible idea to me. It gave her life stability – she led a pretty nomadic life for such a long time. The cottage was a new beginning for her; she found work in the village, and regained her old confidence which had been eroded after the death of her brother Mark. The recipes she has chosen for me are typical of her wide-ranging interests and experiences – Jayesh, an ex-boyfriend, and his sister Sangeeta educated her in the ways of Indian cooking, and a three-month trip around the world when she finished her 'A' levels introduced her to a wide range of international cultures.

MUSHROOM CURRY
with Spiced Rice

SERVES 2

Rachel learnt a lot about cooking curries when she was going out with Jayesh. Mushrooms, although fairly uncommon in India, are a favourite curry ingredient for Rachel and many other Emmerdale curry fans.

1oz (30g) butter or ghee	*1tsp ground cumin*
1 large onion, finely sliced	*2tsp ground coriander*
1 clove garlic, crushed	*1/2tsp ground turmeric*
1 small piece root ginger, peeled and very finely chopped	*2 bay leaves*
	8oz (225g) mushrooms, sliced
1/2tsp ground ginger	*1/2tsp salt*
	6fl oz (175ml) water

FOR THE SPICED RICE

2tbsp oil	*6oz (175g) easy-cook long-grain rice*
1 medium onion, finely sliced	*3/4pt (430ml) water*
1/2tsp caraway seeds	*1/2tsp salt*
1tbsp poppy seeds	*1 1/2oz (45g) pistachios or walnuts, roughly chopped*
2 pieces star anise	
1tsp green cardamoms	

Cook the onion, garlic and ginger in the butter or ghee until soft, then add all the spices and cook for a further 1 minute over a low heat, stirring all the time. Stir in the sliced mushrooms, then add the salt and the water. Simmer for 20 minutes, until the mushrooms are cooked and soft and the curry has thickened. Serve with chutney and spiced rice.

To make the spiced rice: Cook the onion in the oil until soft then add the spices and cook for a further minute or so, stirring all the time over a low heat. Add the rice and stir well to coat the grains with the oil. Add the water to the pan and bring slowly to the boil then stir the rice briefly. Cover and simmer for 15 minutes then remove the pan from the heat and leave for 5 minutes. Fork the nuts through the rice then serve with any curry of your choice.

ROAST CHICORY
with Pine Nuts and Parmesan

SERVES 2

When you don't buy meat you can afford some of the more expensive vegetables such as chicory which is one of Rachel's favourites. Serve with a tomato and cucumber salad.

3 heads of chicory	*black pepper*
1tsp lemon juice	*2tbsp fruity olive oil*
1 small onion, finely sliced	*1tbsp pine kernels*
	1tbsp grated Parmesan cheese
salt and freshly ground	

Preheat the oven to 200°C/400°F/Gas 6. Trim the bases of the chicory then place them in a pan of cold water with the lemon juice. Bring to the boil, simmer for 5 minutes then drain and refresh the chicory in cold water. Cut the heads in half lengthways and place them, cut side down, in a suitable baking tin or dish.

Scatter the onion over the chicory and season well with salt and pepper then spoon the olive oil over. Roast in the oven for 45 minutes. Top the chicory with the pine kernels and cheese then cook very quickly under a hot grill, until the nuts are lightly toasted and the cheese is just melting. Serve immediately.

QUICK
VEGETABLE CHOP SUEY

SERVES 2

This simple but filling dish can be served as part of a Chinese meal or as a main course, just by itself. This quantity of noodles that Rachel uses for just herself, or if serving it with other dishes as part of a meal – allow one sheet of noodles per person for a main course. Don't chop the vegetables up too small – you will rely on them for texture.

2tbsp groundnut oil	*3tsp dry sherry or rice wine*
1 onion, diced	
1 clove garlic, sliced	*4tbsp light soy sauce*
1 carrot, cut into matchsticks	*1 sheet thread egg noodles*
1 small pepper, red or green, seeded and sliced	*1 handful beansprouts – about 2oz (60g)*
1 stick celery, sliced	*freshly chopped coriander to garnish (optional)*
6oz (175g) white cabbage, chopped	

Heat the oil in a large frying-pan or wok, add the prepared onion, garlic, carrot, pepper and celery and cook for 5 minutes, until well softened. Add the cabbage with the sherry and soy sauce then cover the pan and simmer the vegetables for 10 minutes.

Soak the noodles in boiling water for 3 minutes, or as directed, whilst the vegetables are simmering. Drain the noodles and add them to the pan with the beansprouts, toss well, then simmer for a further 2 minutes to soften the beansprouts.

Serve the chop suey garnished with coriander.

HOT BEANS

SERVES 2

Hot Beans may be made with French, fine or runner beans, but cut them finely to allow them to cook quickly and to absorb the flavour of the spicy gravy.

1tbsp groundnut oil
1 clove garlic, finely sliced
1 small green chilli, finely shredded
1tsp ground coriander

¹/2tsp 5-spice powder
8oz (225g) green beans, in 2in (5cm) lengths
3fl oz (90ml) water
1tbsp light soy sauce

Cook the garlic, chilli and spices in the oil for 2–3 minutes, then add the beans and toss them in the mixture. Stir in the water then bring the mixture to the boil. Cover and simmer for 5–8 minutes, until the beans are just soft. Add the soy sauce then serve.

CHEESY-TOPPED SEASONAL VEGETABLES

SERVES 4

Entertaining when you are a vegetarian is a challenge – what to give meat-eating friends that will fill them up! Rachel also has to watch the pennies so this is one of her favourite dishes to prepare for friends – she uses whatever vegetables are cheap and in season.

2lb (900g) prepared vegetables
1¹/2lb (680g) potatoes
2oz (60g) butter or margarine
2oz (60g) flour
1pt (570ml) milk

salt, freshly ground black pepper and dry mustard to taste
3–4oz (90–120g) Cheddar cheese, grated

Preheat the oven to 200°C/400°F/Gas 6. Place the prepared vegetables in a large pan of water, bring to the boil then cook for 10 mins. Drain and place the vegetables in a suitable ovenproof dish. Peel the potatoes and cut them into halves. Bring to boil in a pan of water and boil for 5–10 minutes, according to size. Drain and cool slightly, then slice the potatoes and arrange them in a layer over the vegetables.

Make a cheese sauce. Melt the butter in a pan, add the flour and stir quickly over a low heat for about 30 seconds. Gradually add the milk, stirring thoroughly between each inclusion – if you add the milk too quickly the sauce will go lumpy. Bring the sauce to the boil and cook for 30–60 seconds. Add half the cheese then season to taste with salt, pepper and mustard. Spread the sauce over the vegetables and top with the remaining grated cheese.

Bake the vegetable gratin in the preheated oven for about 30 minutes, until the top is golden brown. Serve with a green salad.

Hotten Juicy

Joe Sugden was one of the first people I met when I came to live and work in Emmerdale. We were in competition for the same job, and I got it. This rather soured our relationship for a while – I think Joe resented me, which was quite understandable. But we became friends in the end, several years later. It's rather strange the way his life has turned out – in those days, Jack was the Sugden with wanderlust. He'd arrive at Emmerdale Farm out of the blue, settle down for a while, muck in at the farm and then be off again without a word. Joe was the brother who stayed at home and looked after the family. Always reliable, always there. I felt sorry for him, although he wouldn't thank me for saying so. He had earned himself a reputation as something of a ladykiller, and his relationships were the subject of endless speculation and gossip throughout the village. I think he was really rather lonely, and craved companionship. After all, most of his affairs were serious matters. They were never brief, and he nearly always ended up setting up home with the objects of his affection. I remember he was quite taken with Ruth Pennington, the vet who lived in Emmerdale for a while. She went to Ireland when an old flame came back into her life and asked her to marry him. Joe tried his best to change her mind, but it wasn't to be. Karen Moore was another visitor to the area

who fell for Joe's charms. She was also interested in his older brother and ended up dating Jack – after she'd finished with Joe. Neither brother was very keen to talk about the situation after Karen left Yorkshire – hardly surprising really.

Joe met Kate Hughes in a supermarket in Hotten, and that's when his problems really started. She moved into the farm with her two children, Mark and Rachel. Joe and Kate married a year later. Unfortunately another member of the family followed them…Kate's jealous ex-husband, who attempted to shoot Joe at close range with a shotgun. It was only thanks to some fast talking from Kate that he wasn't killed. Joe gallantly tried to hush up the story, but it wasn't long before the entire village was talking about it. There was worse to come, though. Kate was sent to prison after she knocked down and killed Pete Whiteley in a drink-driving accident. Joe's life was turned upside down, but he struggled to maintain his happy-go-lucky façade for the sake of Mark and Rachel. It was during this turbulent time that he found himself growing closer to Kim Tate. An afternoon together at a hunt and a drink in The Woolpack led to an illicit kiss. It all ended with Kim telling Joe that she was in love with her husband. An embarrassed Joe decided to take himself off to France to make some sort of sense of his life, and to this day only a few people are aware of the real reason why Joe fled Yorkshire so suddenly.

Kate only returned briefly to Emmerdale Farm when she was released from prison;

the ex-husband of the victim's killer? It was hardly destined to succeed! Joe left Emmerdale and moved to Spain because he felt that the Sugdens had become cursed. But fate was against him; the village was shocked beyond belief when we heard about his fatal car crash. I just can't believe that he'll never walk into The Woolpack again and order a pint of his favourite beer.

the marriage was over as far as she was concerned. I spent many a long evening with Joe trying to make him see that the Kate who came out of prison was a different person to the Kate that went in.

After the divorce Joe lost some of his sense of purpose in life. I know what it's like to love someone and lose them. I'm sure his brief affair with Lynn Whiteley was an attempt to put Kate and the past behind him. He and Lynn were an unlikely combination. The wife of the murder victim and

BREAKFAST WITH THE McALLISTERS

Bernard and Angharad McAllister always said that breakfast was the most important meal of the day; it was vital to start the day off on the right foot. For a few years, when Luke and Jessica were younger, the family would rise early, and Angharad and Bernard took it in turns to prepare a hearty breakfast. Unfortunately, as the two children grew into their teens, getting up early in the morning became an apparently impossible task for them, and the family breakfast turned into a battle zone. Angharad admitted that she was secretly pleased when the early morning family get-together ceased – she enjoys a simple meal at that time, usually fruit or cereal – and as a GP Bernard knew that fried plate-fuls of food aren't the healthiest meals, so the 'big breakfast' was relegated to treat status. Every once in a while the family sits down to one – which is the way it should be.

COUNTRY KEDGEREE

SERVES 4

This is often regarded as a lunch or supper dish but it is delicious at breakfast-time, especially at the weekends, on the rare occasions when a long, lazy day stretches before the family. This recipe has a fair amount of butter in it but Bernard allows that, telling himself that it is a healthier recipe than his very favourite version which includes double cream!

8oz (225g) easy-cook long-grain rice	*3 eggs, size 2 or 3*
salt and freshly ground black pepper	*3oz (90g) butter*
	1 large onion, finely sliced
8oz (225g) smoked haddock, skinned	*1–2tbsp freshly chopped parsley*

Measure the rice in a container then place it in a pan with twice its volume of water and a pinch of salt. Bring to the boil, cover then simmer for 12 minutes, or as directed on the packet. Leave covered for 5 minutes off the heat.

Whilst the rice is cooking, poach the haddock in a little water or cook it in a covered dish in the microwave for about 3 minutes on full power. Drain and flake the fish when cooked. Hard-boil the eggs, then shell and chop them.

To complete the kedgeree, melt the butter in a large pan, add the onion and cook slowly until soft-ened but not browned. Add the cooked rice and mix well, then stir in the flaked haddock and the chopped hard-boiled eggs. Season to taste and heat gently until piping hot. Garnish with parsley.

SPECIAL EGGY BREAD

SERVES 4

When there isn't time for a full cooked breakfast but everyone wants something hot the McAllisters often resort to this family favourite and serve it with fried tomatoes or mushrooms.

6 slices bread, crusts cut off	*salt and freshly ground black pepper*
3 eggs, size 3, beaten	*pinch of paprika pepper*
3tbsp milk	*sunflower oil for frying*

Prepare the bread and cut the slices in half. Beat the eggs with the milk and seasonings then dip the bread into the mixture.

Heat a large frying pan with a little oil, then cook the bread until crisp and brown, turning the slices after 1–2 minutes to cook the second side. Keep warm in the oven whilst cooking the remaining slices, then serve with fried tomatoes or mushrooms.

HEARTY OATMEAL PORRIDGE

SERVES 3–4

Porridge made with rolled oats is quick and easy but it lacks the texture of the traditional oatmeal brew. Use medium oatmeal – coarse will take about 1 hour to cook. Porridge should really be stirred with a spurtle, a tapered wooden stick renowned for its stir-ring capabilities – a wooden spoon does the job almost as well!

1pt (570ml) water
2¹/₂oz (75g) medium
  oatmeal

¹/₂–1tsp salt
salt, sugar, milk or
  golden syrup to serve

Place the water, oatmeal and salt in a pan and bring slowly to the boil, stirring constantly. Reduce the heat and simmer the porridge for about 30 minutes, until the oatmeal is softened, swollen and tender. Add a little extra water or milk as necessary, then serve with salt, or with milk and sugar or syrup.

SODA FARLS

SERVES 4

Bernard really enjoys a traditional cooked breakfast, although he certainly does not have one every day. These farls, which are made from a soda bread mixture, can be cooked on a griddle and make a healthy alternative to fried bread with bacon, egg and sausages.

8oz (225g) plain flour
¹/₂tsp salt
1tsp bicarbonate of soda

¹/₄pt (150ml) buttermilk,
  approx

Preheat a griddle or a heavy-based frying-pan – it is ready when you can hold your hand 6in (15cm) above the surface and the heat coming from it feels even.

  Sieve the flour, salt and bicarbonate of soda into a mixing bowl, then add the buttermilk, mixing with a palette knife to form a soft but workable dough. Do not overwork the mixture, or the farls will be heavy. Turn the mixture out onto a lightly floured surface and roll out to a circle about ³/₄in (2cm) thick. Cut into 4 triangles or farls.

  Cook on the griddle for approximately 4–5 minutes on each side, until browned and the mixture can be seen to be cooked at the sides. Serve with bacon and egg.

FRUITY WINTER COMPOTE

SERVES 4

Angharad always likes to have fruit for breakfast and occasionally enjoys a mixture of dried fruits, soaked in orange juice. As in many families she is really the only one who does enjoy this – Bernard has a little to keep the peace but the children think that apricots and prunes are not for them! The compote keeps well in the fridge and heats up easily on cold days when Angharad prefers it warm. Use dried or part-dried (ready-to-eat) fruits.

4oz (120g) dried
  apricots
4oz (120g) dried apple
  rings
4oz (120g) dried pears
  or peaches

4oz (120g) prunes
³/₄pt (430ml) orange
  juice
1tsp freshly grated
  nutmeg
yogurt to serve

Place all the ingredients in a pan and heat slowly until almost boiling. Remove from the heat and leave to soak for about 8 hours, or overnight. Serve small helpings of the fruits, topped with yogurt – try adding a spoonful or two of muesli for a change.

BAKING WITH BERNARD

Luke and Jessica find their father's interest in bread-making rather extraordinary. I must admit it's rather an odd hobby for a GP, but he's often to be found in the kitchen on a lunchtime, or on his day off, apron on, arms rolled up, kneading dough. According to Bernard pummelling large quantities of firm dough is a therapuetic exercise; a wonderful way of relieving stress.

I remember one occasion when Bernard's efforts in the kitchen resulted in puzzlement and frustration for the poor man. Luke and Biff – ever the jokers – waited until he'd returned to work after one of his famous baking sessions. They then removed the trays of bread from the oven, and left impressions of hens' feet on top of each loaf. To this day Bernard has been unable to work out how they got there. 'Marauding chickens' was one wild explanation!

Jessica and Luke scoff at their father's unusual hobby, but they never refuse the offer of a warm slice of freshly buttered new bread.

MALTED GRAIN BREAD

MAKES 2 LARGE LOAVES

The McAllisters are very fond of malted grain, or granary, bread but the Windsors seldom have it in the shop. Bernard fancies his hand as a baker and this is his favourite loaf to bake. The total preparation and cooking time is about 2½ hours, so the bread can easily be made in an evening.

1oz (30g) fresh yeast	*14oz (400g) strong*
1½pt (850ml) warm	*plain flour*
water	*1tbsp salt*
2.2lb (1kg) bag malted	*3tbsp olive oil*
grain or granary flour	

Crumble the yeast into ½pt (280ml) of the water then leave it to stand for 3–4 minutes before stirring to completely dissolve the yeast. (If you prefer to use easy-blend yeast add 2 sachets of it directly to the flour and omit this stage.)

Mix the flours and salt together in a large bowl and make a well in the centre. Add the oil, the yeast liquid and sufficient of the remaining water to give a soft, manageable dough. Turn out onto a floured surface and knead thoroughly for about 10 minutes, until smooth and elastic. Return the dough to the bowl, cover and leave in a warm place for about 45 minutes, until doubled in size.

Turn the dough out onto a floured surface again and knead lightly – this is known as 'knocking back'. Divide the dough and shape it to fit into two 2lb (900g) loaf tins. Cover the tins and leave in a warm place for a further 30 minutes, or until the dough has risen to the top of the tins.

Preheat the oven to 220°C/425°F/Gas 7. Bake the loaves in the hot oven for about 45 minutes – turn them out of the tins and tap the bottoms to check if they are cooked – they should sound hollow.

Cool on a wire rack and resist the temptation to eat the bread for at least 30 minutes – hot bread is very indigestible!

BARA BRITH

MAKES 1 LARGE LOAF

This is the traditional celebratory bread of Wales – a great favourite of Angharad's and all the McAllister family. Bernard makes this when visitors are coming, especially any of his wife's family.

1oz (30g) yeast	*1oz (30g) caster sugar*
¼pt (150ml) warm	*½tsp mixed spice*
water	*1 egg, size 3, beaten*
12oz (340g) strong	*12oz (340g) mixed dried*
plain flour	*fruit including peel*
1tsp salt	*beaten egg and caster*
1oz (30g) butter	*sugar to finish*

Crumble the yeast into the warm water and leave for 2–3 minutes, then stir well to completely dissolve the yeast. Place the flour and salt in a mixing bowl and rub in the butter, then stir in the sugar and spice. Add the yeast liquid to the bowl with the beaten egg and mix to a soft but not sticky dough. Turn out onto a floured surface and knead thoroughly until smooth and elastic – this will take about 10 minutes.

Flatten out the dough and add the dried fruit to it, then work the fruit into the dough to distribute it evenly. Shape the dough into an oval and place it on a floured baking sheet. Cover and leave to rise for about 1½ hours, until doubled in size. The dough takes a long time to rise because of the weight of the fruit.

Preheat the oven to 180°C/350°F/Gas 4. Brush the loaf with a little beaten egg and sprinkle lightly with caster sugar. Bake for 35 minutes, or until the base of the bara brith sounds hollow when tapped, then cool on a wire rack. Serve sliced and buttered.

ANGHARAD'S BANANA BREAD

MAKES 1 LOAF

With a young man like Luke in the house who is constantly hungry, Angharad always tries to ensure that there is a cake in the tin for when he comes home from school. This is not only quick to make but is also an excellent way of using up over-ripe bananas.

4oz (120g) butter or margarine
4oz (120g) caster sugar
2 eggs, size 3, beaten
8oz (225g) self-raising wholewheat flour

pinch of salt
2 ripe bananas, mashed
2oz (60g) raisins

Preheat the oven to 180°C/350°F/Gas 4. Lightly oil a 2lb (900g) loaf tin, lining the base with silicone paper.

Cream the butter and sugar together until pale and fluffy then gradually beat in the eggs. Fold the flour and bananas into the mixture alternately, adding a little warm water if the mixture is too stiff – it should be a soft dropping consistency and the actual consistency will be determined by the size of the bananas. Finally fold in the raisins.

Turn the mixture into the prepared tin and bake in the preheated oven for about 40 minutes, until a skewer inserted into the cake comes out clean.

Allow the banana bread to cool slightly in the tin before turning out onto a wire rack to cool. Dredge with caster sugar before serving.

FAMILY SUPPERS AT THE SURGERY

I always considered Bernard and Angharad to be dear friends. They were new to the village, but we got on from the moment we met. Angharad is a charming woman, and Bernard is a pillar of the community – so we were drawn to one another.

There was only one brief breakdown in our otherwise fine friendship, and that was when Bernard called on me one evening at The Woolpack. He said he was concerned about me, and then rather impertinently asked how much I weighed, and how much I ate and drank. I was astonished. One never asks a woman about her age. Equally, one never asks a gastronome his weight, and I refused to tell him. Bernard was quick to assure me that he had my best interests at heart. He gave me a few pointers on healthy eating, and then invited me to dinner the next night at the cottage. Angharad had prepared a delicious meal – it was cooked with healthy ingredients, and it tasted wonderful. Angharad revealed that she loves rich food and tasty pastries, but a while ago Bernard had advised her to find healthier alternatives – and she did. As a result they find they rarely have to diet. Healthy eating keeps obesity at bay. I think they were both trying to tell me something in

a rather subtle roundabout way. Sadly their advice comes a little late in my case! It's rather like locking the stable door after the horse has bolted.

Thanks to the way they have been brought up, Luke and Jessica are self-sufficient, so their parents know that their children won't starve while they are away. It's always open house at the cottage, and Biff is one of their most frequent visitors. He's renowned for his capacity to eat almost anything set down in front of him, a man after my own heart! Jessica often warns him that his large appetite and enthusiasm for food will land him in trouble. The first time he was invited to dinner with her parents he made quite an impression on Angharad. She thought him greedy, and quite unsuitable for her daughter. On hearing this from a distressed Jessica, Biff told Angharad that if he ate a lot that evening it was because the food was so delicious, he couldn't help it! Angharad quickly revised her opinion of the lad.

Betty Eagleton was another fan of Angharad's culinary skills. During her morning cleaning sessions at the surgery, Betty would always take time off for a cup of tea and a hunt around the kitchen to see what was available in the way of leftovers. A well-timed moan about the misery of having to cook for one, and the sadness of living alone – and bingo! – Angharad was soon loading platefuls of supper remnants into Betty's large bag. It worked every time!

ROASTED STUFFED RED PEPPERS

SERVES 4

This is an ideal weekday supper dish for any household where everyone is out at work or school. Green peppers simply will not work in this dish – they are too crisp and do not roast in the same way as the sweeter, red peppers.

4 red peppers
4oz (120g) pancetta or very thinly cut streaky bacon
2 medium onions, cut
into segments
6–8 tomatoes, quartered
salt and freshly ground black pepper
4tbsp fruity olive oil

Preheat the oven to 200°C/400°F/Gas 6. Cut the peppers in half lengthways and remove the seeds, core and membranes – use a sharp knife to do this as it is best to leave the green top of the core in place, to help the peppers retain their shape during cooking. Place the peppers in a suitable baking tin.

Cook the pancetta or bacon in a frying-pan until it changes colour – this will take about 1 minute. Do not allow it to brown or it will overcook in the oven. Chop the bacon finely – pancetta will probably fall into pieces so there will be no need to chop that.

Arrange the onions and tomatoes in the pepper halves, sandwiching the pancetta or bacon between the layers. Season with salt and pepper and then spoon some olive oil into each pepper. Roast in the preheated oven for about 45 minutes, until the edges of the peppers are beginning to blacken slightly. Serve immediately, topping the peppers with any juices left in the tin.

CORIANDER AND GARLIC SALMON

SERVES 4

Bernard is the typical modern man who enjoys cooking, and he understands that the best ingredients often require very little in the way of elaborate preparation. Having an Aga makes oven-baking the obvious way to cook the salmon.

4 salmon cutlets	1–1¹/₂oz (30–45g) garlic
4tbsp freshly chopped	butter
coriander	

Preheat the oven to 200°C/400°F/Gas 6. Cut four squares of greaseproof paper or foil.

Place a salmon cutlet on each piece of greaseproof then top the fish with the coriander and butter. Form the greaseproof or foil into a package around the fish – the idea is to retain all the juices during cooking. Bake in the hot oven for 20 minutes.

Serve the salmon still in the paper if you have used greaseproof. If you have cooked in foil, unwrap the parcels before serving and spoon the juices over each piece of salmon. Serve with a tossed salad and potatoes or fresh bread.

CHICKEN AND HAM FILO PIE

SERVES 4

A sophisticated variation on an old family favourite! This pie is quick to make using frozen filo pastry, which has a far lower fat content than any of the other pastries.

8oz (225g) ham,	black pepper
chopped	¹/₄pt (150ml) single
10oz (280g) cooked	cream or crème fraîche
chicken, chopped	3 large sheets filo pastry
1 leek, trimmed and	4tbsp extra virgin olive
very finely sliced	oil
salt and freshly ground	sesame seeds (optional)

Preheat the oven to 190°C/375°F/Gas 5. Mix together the cold meats and the leek, season lightly then bind together with the cream.

Cut the filo pastry sheets in half and use two sheets to line a loose-bottomed 8in (20cm) sandwich tin, brushing each piece of pastry with olive oil. Pile the filling into the prepared tin then place the two remaining pieces of pastry over the filling, brushing them with oil. Fold the edges over, then scatter the sesame seeds over the pie if wished. Bake for 40 minutes, until the pastry is browned and crisped.

BACON AND COCKLE SPAGHETTI

SERVES 4

All the McAllisters love pasta and many of their dishes show a Mediterranean influence. In this dish, one of Bernard's own creations, he mixes a traditional English seafood, cockles, with a creamy garlic sauce for pasta. Bernard sees nothing wrong in cooking with cream occasionally.

12oz (340g) spaghetti	¹/₂pt (280ml) double
4 rashers of smoked back	cream
bacon, rinded and	salt and freshly ground
chopped	black pepper
1–2 cloves garlic,	2–3tbsp freshly chopped
crushed	parsley
8oz (225g) cockles	

Bring a large pan of salted water to the boil then cook the spaghetti as directed. Meanwhile, fry the bacon until browned then add the garlic and cockles with the cream. Bring to the boil and cook until the cream has reduced and become slightly browned in colour and nutty in flavour. Season the sauce with salt and pepper to taste and add the chopped parsley.

Drain the spaghetti, toss it in the sauce until evenly coated and serve immediately on warm plates.

AUBERGINE AND COURGETTE CRACKED WHEAT PILAF

SERVES 4

This is a favourite vegetarian dish of the McAllisters, although some chopped cold meat from the weekend roast could be added. Using cracked wheat makes a welcome change from the more usual supper dishes of this type made with rice.

3tbsp olive oil	8oz (225g) cracked
2 large onions, finely	wheat (bulgar)
sliced	14oz (400g) can
1 clove garlic, crushed	chopped tomatoes with
1 aubergine, trimmed	herbs
and sliced	1/2pt (280ml) stock
2 courgettes, trimmed	salt and freshly ground
and sliced	black pepper

Cook the onions in the oil in a large frying-pan until soft, then add the garlic and aubergine. Cover the pan and cook slowly for 5 minutes or so, until the aubergine starts to soften. Add the courgettes and cracked wheat and stir well, then add the chopped tomatoes and stock. Season lightly.

Bring the mixture to the boil, then cover and simmer for 15 minutes. Stir well, add extra seasoning to taste and then serve with a side salad.

FRESH FIGS
with Yoghurt and Honey

SERVES 4

The McAllisters are not big pudding eaters but they do enjoy some fresh fruit after a meal. This takes virtually no time to prepare and is a lovely way to enjoy fresh figs in season.

4 fresh figs, quartered	4tsp clear honey
4tbsp thick natural	
yogurt	

Arrange the figs on individual plates with the yogurt to one side. Drizzle the honey over the yogurt then serve immediately. Scoop the pink flesh from the figs and eat it with the yogurt.

LEMON MASCARPONE PUDDING

SERVES 4

This is a treat pudding, to be enjoyed only after a light main course such as the Aubergine and Courgette Pilaf. Mascarpone is a very rich soft cheese – Italians eat it mixed with candied peel and glacéd fruits. This is a half healthy recipe!

4oz (120g) sultanas	7fl oz (200ml) crème
1 lemon, grated rind	fraîche
and juice	ginger biscuits for
9oz (250g) mascarpone	serving
2oz (60g) caster sugar	

Soak the sultanas in the lemon juice whilst preparing the rest of the dessert. Beat the mascarpone with the grated lemon rind, then stir in the sugar and crème fraîche and the sugar and mix well. Add the sultanas and the lemon juice then serve in individual dishes.

QUICK CARAMELISED ORANGES

SERVES 4

A quick and easy version of a classic recipe, suitable for mid-week eating in a busy household. The McAllisters have an Aga, so they actually bake the oranges for about 10 minutes in the top of their hot oven – it is quicker and easier under a grill.

4 sweet oranges	2oz (60g) demerara
	sugar

Cut the peel and pith from the oranges using a serated edged knife. Cut off the tops and bottoms of the fruits, then trim away all the white pith, following the contour of the oranges. Slice the oranges and arrange the pieces in a flameproof dish.

Preheat the grill until very hot. Scatter the sugar evenly over the oranges then grill them quickly for just 2–3 minutes, until the sugar has melted and caramelised. Serve immediately.

THE GLOVERS AT ANNIE'S COTTAGE

Jan Glover is a woman who juggles family life with great aplomb, but it hasn't always been like that. When the family first moved into the little cottage owned by Annie Sugden, Jan couldn't find work and it was getting her down. Once the children were off to school on a morning, and Dave and Ned had gone to work, Jan felt the day stretching before her. For years the Glovers had worked their own farm, but they'd fallen on hard times and were forced to sell up. It took Jan a long time to get used to the fact that they'd lost everything they'd cherished and worked for, and she'll never forget the time when all five of them lived in a tiny, cold caravan. The stove had only two gas rings, and preparing meals for the family was no mean feat, but Jan managed it and there were never any complaints about her cooking. Every meal-time, she'd cross her fingers and hope that there would be enough gas in the bottle to cook the food. Somehow they got through the despair, and now the family can look back at that miserable time and laugh.

Jan struck me as a clever, independent sort, so I was glad to give her bar work at The Woolpack. News of her reliability must have spread, because no sooner had she accepted my offer she was asked by Sarah to become little Victoria's childminder. Now she has two careers – three if you include the running of a large household.

Several of the recipes Jan has given me were favourites when the Glovers were living rough, and they're still appreciated today. Although Jan is never frugal with her cooking, the legacy of those impoverished days is such that no food is ever wasted in the Glover household, and everything is used or recycled. We could all do well to follow her example. Husband Ned, a typical Yorkshire farmer, prefers simple, traditional meals – a bit like Jack Sugden – but Jan has consulted Sarah and between them they're both trying to educate their husbands' palettes. As you'll see from the following recipes, I think they're probably succeeding in their mission.

MACARONI CHEESE

SERVES 4–5

It's hard to improve on a family favourite like macaroni cheese, but Jan has a very special way of preparing it which turns a relatively humble dish into a feast.

12oz (340g) short-cut macaroni	1pt (570ml) milk
1 large onion, cut into 8 segments	4oz (120g) Cheddar cheese, grated
2oz (60g) butter or margarine	salt and freshly ground black pepper
2oz (60g) flour	pinch of paprika
	4 tomatoes, quartered

Preheat the oven to 200°C/400°F/Gas 6. Cook the macaroni and onion in a large pan of boiling salted water for 18 minutes, or as directed on the packet. Meanwhile, prepare the cheese sauce. Melt the butter in a separate pan, stir in the flour and cook for 1 minute, stirring all the time. Remove from the heat and gradually stir in the milk, then heat gently, stirring all the time, until boiling and thickened. Season with salt, pepper and a pinch of paprika, then add just over half the grated cheese. Stir in the tomatoes, then pour the whole lot into a suitable ovenproof dish and top with the remaining cheese.

Bake in the preheated oven for 30 minutes, until bubbling and browned, then serve with a side salad. Any left-overs are delicious when reheated – the top of the macaroni becomes crispy and is delicious with tomato ketchup!

BOILED BACON
with Mushroom and Parsley Sauce

SERVES 6

Jan always buys a big bacon joint as it gives useful cold meat for sandwiches and to serve with baked potatoes. When hot, she always serves a mushroom and parsley sauce. Pease pudding is a family favourite when served with the bacon joint.

bacon joint
2oz (60g) butter
8oz (225g) mushrooms,
    finely sliced
2¹/2oz (75g) flour
    (increase this to 3oz
    (90g) if the

mushrooms produce a
    lot of juice)
1pt (570ml) milk
salt and freshly ground
    black pepper
2tbsp freshly chopped
    parsley

Boil the bacon joint allowing 25 minutes per 1lb (460g). Place it in a large pan with water to cover and bring to the boil. Skim off the scum, then simmer the joint for the allotted time.

Just before the joint is cooked prepare the mushroom and parsley sauce. Melt the butter in a pan, add the mushrooms and cook for 4–5 minutes, until soft. Stir in the flour, adding the extra amount if the mushrooms have produced a great deal of juice – you will need the extra flour to thicken the sauce. Cook the mixture over a low heat for 1 minute, to cook the flour. Gradually stir the milk into the sauce off the heat, then bring gently to the boil, stirring all the time. Season the sauce to taste, then add the parsley just before serving.

Cut the skin away from the bacon then slice the joint thinly. Serve with the sauce poured over the meat.

CHINESE-STYLE CHICKEN RISOTTO

SERVES 5

There's never enough meat left on a chicken carcase at Annie's cottage to make another meal as cold meat, but chopped up, with lots of vegetables and nuts and raisins, it makes a very substantial Chinese-style rice dish.

3tbsp oil	*1½pt (850ml) vegetable*
1 large onion, finely	*or chicken stock*
sliced	*1lb (450g) packet frozen*
1 clove garlic, crushed	*mixed Chinese*
12oz (340g) long-grain	*vegetables*
rice	*4oz (120g) salted*
8oz (225g) cooked	*peanuts*
chicken, shredded	*3–4tbsp soy sauce*

Heat the oil in a large frying-pan, add the onion and garlic and cook until soft, then add the rice and fry it until transparent. Stir in the chicken then add the stock and bring to the boil. Cover and simmer slowly for 15 minutes.

Stir the frozen vegetables into the pan and cook for a further 5 minutes. Toss in the peanuts then add soy sauce to taste. Stand, covered, for a few minutes then serve.

LAMB AND LEEK COBBLER

SERVES 4–5

A small half shoulder of lamb makes a filling meal for the Glover family. During the winter months it's just what Ned needs after a hard day down at Emmerdale Farm. Jan likes to dice the meat and then use the bone to make a fresh stock for the casserole.

blade half shoulder of	*6 peppercorns*
lamb, weighing about	*2 bay leaves*
2lb (900g)	*small bunch fresh thyme,*
1lb (460g) leeks, trimmed	*or 1tsp dried*
and thickly sliced	

FOR THE TOPPING

8oz (225g) self-raising	*2oz (60g) hard*
flour	*margarine or butter*
pinch of salt	*1tsp caraway seeds*
	¼pt (150ml) milk

Cut all the meat away from the bone. Place the bone with the leek trimmings and seasonings in a saucepan, add water to cover and boil, in the open pan, for 30 minutes. Strain and reserve the stock, discarding the bone, trimmings and seasonings.

Preheat the oven to 180°C/350°F/Gas 4. Dice the lamb and fry it in a non-stick frying-pan until browned on all sides – using a non-stick pan means that no extra fat is required for the frying process. Transfer the meat to an ovenproof casserole dish. Cut the leeks into ½in (1.25cm) slices and cook them until soft in the lamb fat left in the frying pan; add extra fat if necessary but do try not to as a much better end result will be achieved without. Add the leeks to the lamb in the casserole dish with 1pt (570ml) of the lamb stock. Cover and cook in the preheated oven for 1–1½ hours.

Prepare the cobbler topping towards the end of the cooking time. Mix together the flour and salt and rub in the margarine or butter until the mixture resembles fine breadcrumbs. Stir in the caraway seeds and mix to a soft but workable dough with the milk. Knead lightly on a floured surface, then roll out and cut into 8–10 pieces.

Remove the casserole from the oven and increase the temperature to 200°C/400°F/Gas 6. Season the lamb if necessary, then arrange the scones on top of the meat. Cook for a further 15 minutes, uncovered, in the hot oven. Serve with carrots or mashed swedes.

SAUSAGE AND ONION HOTPOT

SERVES 5

Jan feels that you just can't beat the good old tried and tested recipes when it comes to feeding the family on a shoestring. This has been a Glover family favourite for years – simple, straightforward and delicious.

1½lb (680g) sausages	*salt and black pepper*
3 large onions, finely	*3 medium potatoes,*
sliced	*weighing about 1¼lb*
14oz (400g) can	*(570g)*
chopped tomatoes	*1oz (30g) butter, melted*

Preheat the oven to 200°C/400°F/Gas 6. Fry the sausages until browned all over then transfer them to an ovenproof casserole dish. Cook the onions in the fat from the sausages until they are browned, then add them to the casserole dish with a little salt and pepper and the chopped tomatoes. Cover and cook in the preheated oven for 45 minutes.

Meanwhile peel the potatoes and cut them into

halves. Boil them for 10 minutes, then drain and allow them to cool. Slice the potatoes and arrange them over the top of the sausages and tomato. Brush with melted butter and cook, uncovered, for a further 40 minutes in the oven. Serve with freshly cooked vegetables.

If the Glovers spent the best part of last year wondering where the next morsel of food was going to come from, they've certainly come a long way. When Dave became gamekeeper at Home Farm Estate, one of the perks of the job was the occasional piece of game, the odd rabbit. Even Ned enjoys the goodwill of his boss, Jack Sugden, who always gives the labourer chicken and lamb when he can. Annie's Aga, taken out of the old Emmerdale Farm building and now in her small cottage, has worked overtime since the Glovers moved in.

RABBIT IN CIDER WITH PRUNES

SERVES 4–5

When Roy bags a rabbit the Glovers are half way to their favourite meal, and having one of the main ingredients for nothing means that they can afford some cider for the pot. Rabbit isn't to everyone's taste but this recipe really is delicious – do try it!

1 rabbit, skinned and jointed	2tbsp cider vinegar
2tbsp seasoned flour	salt and freshly ground black pepper
3tbsp oil	3/4pt (440ml) sweet cider
2 onions, sliced	vegetable or chicken stock
2 carrots, thickly sliced	6 cloves
2 medium parsnips, thickly sliced	2tbsp freshly chopped herbs
6oz (175g) pitted prunes	

Toss the rabbit in the seasoned flour then brown it in the oil in a large pan. Remove the rabbit from the pan, add the onions and cook until soft. Stir in the carrots and parsnips and cook for a minute or so with the onions, then return the rabbit to the pan and add the prunes. Pour the vinegar over the meat, then season with salt and pepper and add the cider with enough stock to almost cover the rabbit. Toss in the remaining seasonings then bring the casserole to the boil. Cover the pan and simmer the rabbit slowly for 45 minutes – 1 hour, until tender.

Remove the rabbit and vegetables to a serving plate then boil the juices rapidly until reduced slightly to make a sauce. Season as necessary then spoon the sauce over the rabbit and serve with freshly cooked green vegetables and potatoes.

BRAISED OXTAIL IN BEER

SERVES 3–4

Oxtail is good homely fare in Emmerdale – down south it has become the trendy food of chic bistros and restaurants. Jan cooks oxtail in a little of The Woolpack's Emmerd Ale which gives it a marvellous flavour. Not all the young Glovers will eat oxtail but Jan and Ned love it, so it is often an evening-in treat for them.

2tbsp seasoned flour	Emmerd Ale or other beer
2tsp mustard powder	
4–6 pieces oxtail	salt and freshly ground black pepper
1oz (30g) lard	
2 onions, sliced	3 bay leaves
2 large carrots, sliced	8 cloves
18fl oz (500ml)	1 cinnamon stick, broken

Preheat the oven to 160°C/325°F/Gas 3. Mix together the seasoned flour and the mustard, then coat the oxtail pieces liberally in the mixture. Melt the lard in a flameproof casserole, add the oxtail and brown on all sides over a high heat. Remove the meat from the casserole then stir the onions into the hot fat and cook until they are soft. Return the oxtail to the pan then add the carrots and beer and bring gently to the boil. Add all the seasonings, then cover the casserole and transfer it to the preheated oven for 3 hours. Remove the bay and cinnamon, season to taste and serve the oxtail with lots of creamy mashed potato.

Jan actually prefers to leave oxtail to stand overnight before reheating and serving it. All the fat from the casserole then hardens in a layer over the meat and can be removed. This resting period allows the flavours to really blend together to make a truly memorable dish.

RICE AND RAISIN PUDDING

SERVES 4–5

Do you like the skin or not? There's always a fight over it in the Glovers' house! This traditional pudding is made a little bit more special by adding a few seedless raisins.

3oz (90g) pudding rice
2oz (60g) seedless
  raisins
1¹/₂oz (45g) caster sugar

1pt (570ml) milk
knob of butter
nutmeg

14¹/₂oz (411g) can
  apricot halves
15oz (432g) can
  pineapple chunks
6oz (175g) plain flour

3oz (90g) butter or block
  margarine
2oz (60g) demerara
  sugar

Preheat the oven to 150°C/300°F/Gas 2. Place the rice, raisins and sugar in an 1¹/₂pt (850ml) ovenproof dish and pour the cold milk over them. Dot with a few flakes of butter and scatter a little nutmeg over the top – freshly grated is best. Cook slowly in the preheated oven for 2 hours, stirring once during cooking. Serve with a knob of jam, if you like.

ANNIE'S SPECIAL BREAD AND BUTTER PUDDING

SERVES 5–6

The biggest drawback to bread and butter pudding is that any fruit on top tends to burn and become bitter. In this special recipe the fruit is all hidden away inside along with the marmalade, her secret ingredient. Jan likes to leave the pudding to stand for 30 minutes or so before baking, if possible, to allow the bread to soak up the milk.

6 large slices of bread
butter
4tbsp orange
  marmalade
4oz (120g) mixed cake
  fruit

3 eggs, size 3, beaten
1¹/₂oz (45g) caster sugar
³/₄pt (430ml) milk
few drops of vanilla
  essence

Preheat the oven to 190°C/375°F/Gas 5. Lightly butter an ovenproof dish. Spread the bread with butter (or margarine, if you prefer) and marmalade. Arrange half the bread in the bottom of the dish, then cover with a layer of the fruit and top with the remaining bread, marmalade side up. Beat the eggs and sugar together then add the milk and vanilla essence. Pour the custard over the bread and bake in the preheated oven for 30–40 minutes, until set. Cool slightly before serving.

APRICOT AND PINEAPPLE CRUMBLE

SERVES 6

The Glover men like their puddings, and they have to be filling to satisfy their appetites. This crumble is a winter dessert and is made with canned fruits from the Windsors' shop.

Preheat the oven to 200°C/400°F/Gas 6. Drain the fruit juices into a small saucepan and place the fruits in an ovenproof dish, mixing them together. Rub the butter into the flour until the mixture resembles fine breadcrumbs, then stir in the sugar and spoon the crumble over the fruit. Bake in the preheated oven for 30–40 minutes, until browned. Serve with custard and the warmed fruit juices.

ANNIE IN SPAIN

Annie's first trip to Spain turned out to be something of a revelation for her. Until she hit her early seventies, foreign trips were rare. She'd never had any inclination to go to Spain; it was Amos who persuaded her. She'd been out there for only two days when she decided she could easily live there permanently. It wasn't difficult to work out why; she like the slow and easy pace of life, and the climate was warm. Annie was seventy-two, and she'd risen at the crack of dawn every morning for as long as she could remember; she was always the last one to lock up the farmhouse and go to bed. The winters were cold, and she rarely had time to enjoy the summer.

The decision to move to Spain wasn't difficult.

A new way of life meant having to adjust to new ways of cooking, and she rose to the challenge as only Amos knew she would. Living so close to the sea it was sensible to take advantage of the local fish and sea food, and before long, Annie's Paella had become a much-talked-about sensation. But although she immersed herself in traditional Spanish cookery, she never really lost her love of English food. What she did (and very successfully, too) was to take her basic English recipes and adapt them, incorporating Mediterranean produce and Spanish methods. You can't teach an old dog new tricks? Nonsense.

EASY PAELLA

SERVES 4

Since Annie moved to Spain she has enjoyed experimenting with the local cuisine. Paella is a classic Spanish dish, but it certainly wouldn't be possible to get all the fresh ingredients needed in the shop in Emmerdale. Annie has adapted this recipe to send to her friends at home.

1 Spanish onion, finely sliced
2tbsp olive oil
8oz (225g) boneless chicken, diced
4 squid tubes, cut into rings
8oz (225g) chorizo sausage, sliced
1tsp Spanish paprika
1/4pt (150ml) dry white wine
8oz (225g) easy-cook long-grain rice
12fl oz (340ml) stock

14oz (400g) can chopped tomatoes with peppers
salt and freshly ground black pepper
8oz (225g) fresh mussels in their shells
6oz (175g) peeled prawns
14oz (400g) can artichoke hearts, drained and cut into halves
freshly chopped parsley to garnish

Cook the onion in a large pan in the olive oil until soft, then increase the heat, add the diced chicken and cook until browned on all sides (this will take about 5 minutes). Stir in the prepared squid, chorizo and paprika and cook quickly until the squid is firm and white, then pour in the wine and cook until it has reduced by about half. Add the rice, stock,

chopped tomatoes and seasoning. Bring to the boil then cover and simmer for 15 minutes.

Clean the mussels by scraping off any scale and pulling away any beards. Add the mussels with the prawns and artichokes and cook for a further 3–4 minutes, stirring once or twice, until the mussels have opened. Leave the paella, covered, for 5 minutes, then add any seasoning that is required and serve garnished with chopped parsley.

SPANISH STUFFED SHOULDER OF LAMB

SERVES 6–8

After many years in Emmerdale Annie's favourite meat is still lamb, despite all the exciting foods that she now cooks with in Spain. This is her version of a classic dish served at Easter throughout Spain.

4oz (120g) mushrooms, finely chopped
1oz (30g) butter
1tbsp lemon juice
1tsp paprika
1lb (460g) pork sausagemeat
1 clove garlic, crushed
6tbsp sherry
2tbsp freshly chopped herbs
salt and black pepper
1 shoulder of lamb, completely boned out

Preheat the oven to 180°C/350°F/Gas 4. Cook the mushrooms in the butter with the lemon juice and paprika for about 5 minutes, until they are soft. Mix with the sausagemeat, garlic, sherry and herbs, then season with salt and pepper.

Open out the lamb on a board and season it lightly. Pack the stuffing into the lamb, then draw the meat up around the filling and tie or truss with string, to keep the stuffing enclosed during cooking. Place the stuffed joint in a roasting tin.

Roast the lamb in the oven for 1–1¼ hours, until

the meat is cooked through and the juices run clear when a skewer is inserted into the meat. Stand for 10 minutes before carving – which is very easy as this is a totally boneless joint.

ESCABECHE OF FISH

SERVES 4

This is a very typically Spanish dish of preserved fish. It is best prepared a day or two in advance so Annie often makes it when visitors are coming, especially anyone from Emmerdale who might be delayed on their journey.

1lb (460g) thick haddock fillet, skinned	*1 green pepper, seeded and diced*
3–4tbsp olive oil	*salt and freshly ground black pepper*
1 Spanish onion, finely sliced	*1/4pt (150ml) white wine vinegar*
1 clove garlic, crushed	*3fl oz (90ml) water*
4oz (120g) mushrooms, sliced	*1/2oz (15g) granulated sugar*

Cut the haddock into bite-sized pieces. Heat 2tbsp of oil in a frying-pan and fry the fish until it is just cooked. Transfer to a suitable serving dish. Heat the remaining oil in the pan, then add the onion and garlic and cook slowly until soft but not browned. Add the mushrooms and pepper and cook for a further 3–4 minutes then spoon the vegetables over the fish and season lightly with salt and pepper.

Pour the vinegar and water into the frying-pan and add the sugar. Bring to the boil, stirring to dissolve the sugar, then pour the hot liquid over the fish and vegetables. Leave to cool, then cover and chill the escabeche in the 'fridge for 24 hours before serving with fresh crusty bread.

HONEYED CITRUS SALAD

SERVES 2

Oranges are so wonderful in Spain – many Spaniards eat them sliced and dressed with a light, fragrant olive oil. This fruit salad is a more conventional serving suggestion – use the best quality honey that you can for the very finest flavour.

2 sweet oranges	*4tbsp clear honey*
1 grapefruit	*demerara sugar for serving*
1–2tbsp lemon juice	

Take the zests from 1 orange and the grapefruit and reserve them for decoration. Cut the peel and pith from all the fruits using a serrated edged knife – follow the contours of the fruits to avoid wastage. Slice the fruits thinly, or remove the flesh in segments from between the membranes. Arrange the fruit in 2 individual dishes.

Mix the lemon juice and honey together and pour them over the fruit, then leave to marinade for at least 1 hour before serving. Offer the demerara sugar separately should anyone want to add sweetness.

Masses of delicious fresh fruit and vegetables can be found in Spain, and Annie has created a wonderful range of recipes which make full use of their refreshing tastes and aromas.

In her previous life in Yorkshire, vegetables were destined for the casserole pot, or accompanied the roast of the day. Fruit such as apples and pears were mere snacks between meals to stave off the hunger pangs. Nowadays, Annie is a champion of fresh fruit and vegetables; she uses them to make wonderful salads, and they often form the basis of a delicious meal. Her Mediterranean diet has given her more energy and a healthier outlook on life. She's not given up her baking completely, though. The Spanish enjoy eating cake – nothing heavy, mind you – they have to be light and fluffy. So if she ever feels homesick, she'll dig out her apron, switch on the oven and bake until she's got it out of her system. Although Amos is concerned when she's in one of her 'down' moods, he's delighted when she pulls herself together: he has both a friend in happier spirits, and a wonderful cake for tea!

Annie's love of life has never been more apparent. She can't imagine returning to Emmerdale, and who can blame her? Besides, she's a different person; few would recognise her. The sherry-drinking lady of old now enjoys good wine and sangria, and a slow walk along the beach at the end of the day.

GLOBE ARTICHOKES
with Garlic Olive Oil

SERVES 2

Spain is an artichoke lovers' paradise! They are so plentiful in the markets, and affordable, that they have become an everyday treat for Annie and Amos. Artichokes are at their best served simply. You might prefer to cook the artichokes without removing the choke, but they will need up to 1 hour to cook.

2 globe artichokes	*4–6tbsp fruity olive oil*
1tbsp lemon juice	*1 small clove garlic,*
freshly ground black	*crushed*
pepper	

Bring a large pan of water to the boil. Trim the stalks and the tops from the leaves of the artichokes. Pull back the leaves until you can see the hairy choke in the centre of the vegetables (trim the leaves back to do this, if necessary) and then carefully remove the choke with a small sharp knife.

Cook the artichokes with the lemon juice in the boiling water for 30 minutes, or until just tender. Drain well, then season lightly with pepper. Mix the oil and garlic together and pour a little into the centre of each artichoke. Pull off the leaves and dip the bases in the dressing, then draw them through your teeth to remove the soft artichoke flesh. Eat the centre of the artichoke, the fond, with any remaining dressing.

HOT POTATO SALAD

SERVES 2

Most of the ingredients in this salad are served cold but the potatoes are added to the dish when they are still hot, just before serving. This salad is a meal in itself as it contains tuna fish, egg and peppers, all favourite Spanish ingredients.

FOR THE DRESSING

6tbsp fruity olive oil	*3tbsp freshly chopped*
1tbsp sherry vinegar	*parsley*
pinch of dry mustard	*1 clove garlic, crushed*
1tsp granulated sugar	*salt and black pepper*

FOR THE SALAD

8 new potatoes, scrubbed	*seeded and sliced*
salad leaves	*1 small yellow pepper,*
3¹/2oz (100g) can tuna,	*seeded and sliced*
flaked	*half a Spanish onion,*
1 small red pepper,	*sliced into rings*
2 hard-boiled eggs, cut	*1tsp capers*
into quarters	

Prepare the dressing by mixing all the ingredients together and seasoning well – it will be a thick, green sauce. Leave until required.

Place the potatoes in a pan of salted water and bring to the boil. Simmer for 10–15 minutes, until just tender, then drain.

Arrange the salad leaves on individual plates, then top with the remaining ingredients. Slice the potatoes thickly and add them to the salad, then toss all the ingredients in the dressing. Serve immediately.

ORANGE
AND ALMOND CAKE

SERVES 6–8

Oranges and almonds are widely used in Spain, where cakes and fresh fruits are the most popular desserts.

4 eggs, size 3, separated	*almonds, very finely*
4oz (120g) caster sugar	*chopped*
grated zest of 1 sweet	*¹/2pt (280ml) fresh*
orange	*orange juice*
2oz (60g) ground	*3oz (90g) demerara*
almonds	*sugar*
2oz (60g) toasted flaked	*1 cinnamon stick*

Preheat the oven to 180°C/350°F/Gas 4, and line a 8in (20cm) deep round cake tin with non-stick baking parchment – this delicate cake is easier to turn out if you have a loose-bottomed cake tin.

Whisk the egg yolks, sugar and orange zest until thick, then whisk in the ground and chopped almonds. Whisk the egg whites until stiff then carefully and quickly fold them into the mixture. Pour into the prepared tin, level the top, then bake in the preheated oven for about 45 minutes, until firm and springy to the touch. Turn out onto a wire rack lined with baking parchment and allow it to cool. When the cake is cold, invert it onto a serving plate and remove the baking parchment – this stops it sticking to the cooling rack. Heat the orange juice, sugar and cinnamon stick, stirring until the sugar is dissolved. Bring to the boil and boil for 3–4 minutes, until slightly syrupy, then remove the cinnamon.

Pierce the surface of the cake repeatedly with a small sharp skewer. Spoon the syrup over the cake, allowing it to soak in and impregnate the sponge. Scatter a few toasted flaked almonds over the cake (this helps to hide the marks of the skewers) and then leave for at least 1 hour before serving.

AMOS ABROAD

For years Amos Brearly and the Yorkshire Dales went arm in arm like love and marriage. After a cold day out in the dales or an afternoon dry-stone-walling, Amos was always on hand at The Woolpack to serve an expert pint and offer dour advice. His downturned mouth and large whiskers were legendary, and so was his love of Emmerdale. Who would have thought that the old man would forsake it all for the ex-pat lifestyle of the Mediterranean? It was a brave decision; since leaving his home town of Bridlington in his youth he'd made the Dales his home. A brief sojourn into Africa during the war had been his only experience of foreign travel. Why did he do it? Well, he told me he could see the way the rest of his life was going. Retirement, annual entry of the Emmerdale Giant Marrow Competition, cold winters and cold summers. Infrequent trips to his old

love – The Woolpack. And he wanted something different. A holiday in Spain opened up his eyes. He found the prospects of warm evenings gazing out over a deep blue sea quite attractive, and on a whim – Amos had never done anything before on a whim – he bought a villa.

He freely admits he's taken to Spanish life like a duck to water. The leisurely pace of it suits him, but his die-hard habits of rising with the Yorkshire dawn have stood him in good stead; instead of shopping for his provisions in the supermarket, the early morning finds him down in the local market where he buys his fish and vegetables fresh. Years ago he wouldn't have entertained European food; now, apart from craving for roast beef and Yorkshire pudding once in a while, his culinary habits have changed beyond belief. Spain has truly given Amos Brearly a new lease of life.

SPANISH BEANS WITH SAUSAGES

SERVES 2–3

When Amos takes over in the kitchen he likes to cook simple foods with robust and gutsy flavours – this traditional Catalan dish is one of his favourites. The casserole may be baked in a slow oven at 160°C/325°F/Gas 3 for 30–40 minutes as an alternative, steam-free method of cooking.

2tbsp fruity olive oil
1 Spanish onion, finely sliced
4 rashers thick cut smoked streaky bacon, rinded and chopped
2 small cloves garlic, peeled but left whole
14oz (400g) can black-eyed beans or similar
salt and freshly ground black pepper
nutmeg
6–8 small chorizo sausages

Cook the onion and bacon together in a flameproof casserole in the oil until just soft. Stir in the garlic and beans with their juice then bring slowly to the boil. Season with salt, pepper and a little freshly grated nutmeg, then add the chorizos. Cover the casserole and simmer slowly for 20–30 minutes, adding a little extra stock or water if necessary – the beans

should be soft and moist but not swimming in lots of liquid. Season well, adding extra nutmeg if necessary, then serve with a green salad.

SPANISH OMELETTE

SERVES 2

Potatoes are very good in Spain – they usually have a waxy texture and lots of flavour. They are the traditional filling for Spanish omelettes, cakes of egg and vegetables which are served sliced into wedges.

3tbsp fruity olive oil
1 Spanish onion, finely sliced
8oz (225g) potatoes, diced
4oz (120g) frozen peas
1 small red pepper, seeded and diced
1tsp olive oil
6 eggs, size 3, beaten
salt and freshly ground black pepper

Heat the olive oil in a 10in (25cm) frying-pan, then add the onion and potato and cook until just soft and lightly golden brown – this will take about 10 minutes. Add the peas and pepper and cook for a further 2–3 minutes, until all the vegetables are soft. Drain off any excess liquid from the pan – the peas and peppers sometimes produce quite a bit of water. Add the extra teaspoon of olive oil, then pour in the eggs,

beaten with some salt and pepper. Cook the omelette for about 5 minutes, until the egg is set, shaking the pan occasionally to prevent the omelette from sticking. Preheat the grill then lightly brown the top of the omelette.

Serve immediately, cut into wedges.

SANGRIA

SERVES 6

Sangria is the famous fruit cup of Spain, consisting of red wine, brandy and plenty of fruits for garnish – rather like a Mediterranean Pimms! Amos has become an expert in mixing sangria and all its variations. Some people add banana to the drink, but Amos finds that it becomes too soft and mushy after a very short time.

1 bottle Rioja	1 peach, peeled and
3–4tbsp brandy, or more	diced
to taste	1 small pear, peeled and
2 lemons	diced
1 small orange, finely	2tbsp demerara sugar
sliced	crushed ice for serving

Mix the wine and brandy together in a large glass jug then add the strained juice of one of the lemons. Slice the remaining lemon very thinly and add it to the wine with the other prepared fruits, then stir in

the sugar, adding a little more or less according to taste. Sangria can be very strong so it may be an idea to add some crushed ice to the jug at this stage, and to let it melt for 20 minutes or so, before adding a little more ice just before serving.

SANGRITA

SERVES 10

When the Spanish returned from Mexico they brought many ideas from the New World home with them. One was for this tomato-based cocktail, traditionally made with very hot peppers but toned down by Amos who uses Spanish paprika in place of the more fiery cayenne or fresh chillis.

2 limes	orange juice
2lb (900g) ripe tomatoes,	3 spring onions, very
skinned, seeded and	finely chopped
chopped, or 17oz	1tsp hot Spanish
(500g) passata (sieved	paprika
tomato pulp)	salt, sugar and chilli
½pt (280ml) fresh	sauce to taste

Squeeze the juice from the limes and place it in a liquidiser or food processor with all the remaining ingredients, then blend until smooth. Add salt and sugar to taste, and a dash of chilli sauce if you like a hotter flavour. Serve with a tequila or vodka chaser.

Hotten Fruity

Annie Sugden, one of the stalwarts of our community, is renowned for her plain speaking and her no-nonsense approach to life. But she's also well known for her generosity, kindness of thought and words of wisdom. When we decided to rename the village of Beckindale, Emmerdale was the perfect choice, in deference to one of its elders and best-loved characters. Annie Sugden, for many years the stern matriarch of Emmerdale Farm, and still formidable in her old age, welcomed the change with a smile and a tear. The name of the family home will now live on through the ages.

As I understand it, Annie is a classic example of the woman who gained her wisdom by watching the activities and listening to the words of others. She rarely travelled during her early years and most of her life was spent at Emmerdale Farm. Yet somehow she managed to become a worldly-wise woman whose opinion has been sought by most in the village and valued by all. Her

marriage to Jacob was not an easy one. She had a tough life; her husband was a hard drinker who showed little interest in the farm. Annie was left to raise a family and run the farm while Jacob drank his life away in The Woolpack. Luckily her three children Peggy, Jack and Joe were prepared to help out as they grew older. Jacob's demise in 1972 was a relief to the family by all accounts.

When I first moved into the area I mistakenly assumed that Annie and Henry Wilks were together – as a couple. They spent a lot of time together; he was a frequent visitor at the farm. However, they very quickly put me straight on a few things when I invited them out to dinner and inquired if they would tie the knot someday. The dinner finished rather earlier than expected! Joe did reveal to me that he and Jack often speculated on their mother's relationship with Henry Wilks. Henry moved up to the farm after he left The Woolpack. Annie admitted that the man had asked for her hand in marriage but she turned him down. If he'd lived... who knows, Annie may have changed her mind eventually and become Annie Wilks!

Instead, she married a man called Leonard Kempinski, which came as a bolt

out of the blue. I know the family were stunned by Annie's announcement, and Jack hardly spoke to her for days. They should have known that something like that was on the cards; her visits to Spain to see Amos had become more frequent. Jack and Joe joked about their mother keeping a 'fancy man' on the Costa Brava, but little did they imagine that it was true! Leonard's death in the air disaster curtailed Annie's travelling for a while. Her grief and her injuries kept her in Yorkshire, but once she had recovered and felt ready to face the world again, she set off on her travels. Annie is now a frequent Mediterranean visitor, and Amos' villa echoes to the sounds of their laughter and conversation.

But Emmerdale is never far away from her thoughts. The cottage she bought with Leonard is still her main home. Family photographs sit atop the old piano which stood for sixty years in the farm parlour. And when Annie is home, the doors are thrown open to all and the new generation of Sugdens mingles with the memories of Sugdens gone.

SUMMER SUNDAY CRICKET

The Emmerdale Cricket Match has been an annual event for as long as anyone can remember. Old Sam Pearson won the great trophy – the Butterworth Bowl – when he was a lad, and that was many, many years ago! Last year, two young village lads – Luke and Biff – were rather scathing of the whole event. They wondered why everyone took the game so seriously. After all, it was 'only a game'. They were soon made to see how important the match is; the reputation of the village is at stake. By the end of the day Luke and Biff were cheering along with the rest of us. In fact they were seen talking to Seth afterwards, asking him to give them cricket lessons (those two must have more money than sense!).

The neighbouring villages all take part. For one day of the year, we Emmerdalers stick to our own; one just does *not* fraternise with the competition. It's a ruthless affair. Some years ago a scandal broke when the Kelthwaite team was accused of bringing in an ex-Somerset player. The *Hotten Courier* was the first to run with the story, but unfortunately for the newspaper it turned out to be nothing more than a vicious rumour spread by one of the other teams. Here at Emmerdale we find we don't have to resort to such devious tactics; the natural talent of our players shines through. Usually – though perhaps not recently . But it's the taking part that's important, not the winning. I tried to tell Eric Pollard that, but he wouldn't listen.

YORKSHIRE TEABREAD

MAKES 1 LOAF

Yorkshire tea is famous throughout England – a strong and distinctive brew. Any cold tea left in the pot can be used to soak the fruit for this teabread, giving a moist, succulent result. Teabread is always welcome at the cricket match – served sliced and buttered it provides a welcome change from cakes and biscuits, and creates less last-minute panics than sandwiches.

6oz (175g) mixed dried fruits	1tbsp marmalade
1/4pt (150ml) cold tea	8oz (225g) self-raising flour, plain or wholewheat
6oz (175g) soft brown sugar	1tsp bicarbonate of soda
2oz (60g) butter or margarine	1tsp mixed spice
	1 egg, size 3, beaten

Preheat the oven to 180°C/350°F/Gas 4 and line a 2lb (900g) loaf tin with baking parchment or greased greaseproof paper.

Place the fruit, tea, sugar, butter and marmalade in a saucepan and heat gently until the butter is melted and the sugar dissolved. Leave to cool slightly.

Sieve the dry ingredients together into a large bowl, make a well in the centre then add the fruit mixture and the beaten egg. Mix together quickly – it will be a very runny mixture and may be slightly frothy from the bicarbonate of soda. Pour into the prepared tin and bake in the preheated oven for about 1 hour, until a skewer inserted into the loaf comes out clean.

Cool the teabread slightly, then turn out onto a wire rack to cool completely. Serve sliced and buttered.

CIDER CAKE

CUTS INTO 18 PIECES

The addition of cider and a little spice to a basic sponge mixture makes a satisfying and more substantial cake. This is a great favourite with the whole Emmerdale team.

6oz (175g) butter or margarine	1tsp cinnamon
6oz (175g) caster or soft brown sugar	pinch of salt
	1/2pt (280ml) cider
3 eggs, size 3, beaten	1 Granny Smith apple, peeled, cored and sliced
12oz (340g) self-raising flour	
1tsp bicarbonate of soda	juice of half a lemon

Preheat the oven to 180°C/350°F/Gas 4 and line a tin about 8x12in (20x30cm) with baking parchment or greased greaseproof paper.

Cream together the butter and sugar until pale and fluffy then gradually add the beaten egg. Sieve together the flour, raising agents, cinnamon and salt and add a little of the mixture to the bowl. Stir in the cider then fold in the remaining flour – the cake mix will resemble a thick batter.

Pour the mixture into the prepared tin and decorate with the apple slices, brushed with lemon juice to prevent browning. Bake the cake in the preheated oven for about 1 hour, until a skewer inserted into the centre of the cake comes out clean. Sprinkle with caster sugar then cool slightly before transferring the cake to a wire rack to cool completely. Cut into 18 pieces.

FIG CAKE

SERVES 8–10

This delicious biscuity cake may also be filled with dates, but perhaps the wives of the Emmerdale cricket team think that figs will give the opposing team more of an off-field problem?! The fig purée may be blended until smooth in a liquidiser, if necessary.

4oz (120g) butter or block margarine	1 egg, size 3, beaten
4oz (120g) caster sugar	12oz (340g) self-raising flour
few drops of vanilla essence	pinch of salt

FOR THE FILLING

8oz (225g) dried figs	1 orange, grated rind and juice
2tbsp clear honey	

Cream the butter and sugar together until pale and fluffy, then beat in the egg and vanilla essence. Add the flour and salt and mix to a stiff dough. Cover with plastic wrap and chill in the fridge for about an hour.

Prepare the filling. Place the figs, honey and orange juice and honey in a pan and cook slowly for 5–10 minutes, until the mixture can be beaten into a thick purée. Remove from the heat and allow to cool.

Preheat the oven to 190°C/375°F/Gas 5. Roll out half the biscuit mixture and use it to line the base of a 8in (20cm) loose-bottomed sandwich tin. Spread it with the figs, then roll out the remaining mixture to fit the tin, prick it with a fork, then place it over the figs. Mark into 8–10 portions with a sharp knife.

Bake for 30 minutes. Mark the top layer again into portions, then allow to cool slightly before removing to a wire rack to cool completely.

YORKSHIRE PARKIN

MAKES 15–18 SQUARES

Where was parkin first made, in Yorkshire or Scotland? It would take a brave Scot to challenge the Yorkshire claim in Emmerdale! Parkin is best made a day or two before it is to be eaten.

A peaceful Sunday afternoon sat in a deckchair, followed by afternoon tea in the pavilion, is my idea of heaven. As for the cricket, well, it's fine on the day; it's the selection process a few weeks earlier which is the cause of all my problems. Joe and Jack Sugden almost came to blows one year when Jack made it onto the team and Joe didn't. They both turned against me – just because I'm on the selection committee. It took several weeks for the rift to heal.

At the end of the day, when egos have been boosted and destroyed and the inter-village rivalry is over, we all shake hands and take a share of the wonderful food that has amassed during the afternoon. Annie Sugden, if she happens to be around, brings her homemade Yorkshire parkin; it always goes down well with the spectators. Kelthwaite and Connelton may disagree as to which is the best village when it comes to cricket, but when it comes to providing a perfect afternoon tea, Emmerdale is the tops!

4oz (120g) clear honey	*8oz (225g) plain flour*
4oz (120g) black treacle	*(use a fine wholemeal*
2oz (60g) soft brown	*if you wish)*
sugar	*6oz (175g) medium*
4oz (120g) butter or	*oatmeal*
block margarine	*1/2tsp bicarbonate of*
1/4pt (150ml) milk	*soda*
2 eggs, size 3, beaten	*2tsp ground ginger*

Preheat the oven to 160°C/325°F/Gas 3 and line a tin about 8x10in (20x25cm) with baking parchment or greased greaseproof paper.

Heat the honey, treacle, sugar and butter together until the butter has melted and the sugar dissolved. Cool slightly, then add the milk and the beaten eggs and mix well. Place all the dry ingredients together in a large bowl, add the treacle mixture and beat until smooth. Pour into the prepared tin and bake in the preheated oven for 1 hour.

ECCLES CAKES

MAKES 12

Commercially made Eccles cakes are often so enormous that they are too big to really enjoy. These are a far better size! Of course, if you have time to make your own flaky or puff pastry they will be even better, but most of the cricket wives and girlfriends use frozen.

FOR THE FILLING

1oz (30g) butter, melted	*4oz (120g) currants*
1oz (30g) soft brown sugar	*2oz (60g) chopped mixed peel*
1tsp mixed spice	

FOR THE PASTRY

1lb (460g) prepared flaky or puff pastry	*milk*
	granulated sugar

Preheat the oven to 220°C/425°F/Gas 7. Mix all the ingredients for the filling together and leave until required.

Roll out the pastry very thinly until you can cut out 12 circles about 4in (10cm) in diameter – use a saucer as a guide. Divide the filling between the 12 circles, then brush the edges of the pastry with water. Gather the pastry together like a purse around the filling, then seal it together with your fingers and turn the Eccles cakes over.

Flatten each cake slightly with your hand, then roll them out thinly to circles about 3in (7.5cm) in diameter – the fruit may break through but don't worry. Make three slashes across each cake with a sharp knife then place them on baking sheets.

Brush the cakes with a little milk then sprinkle each one generously with granulated sugar. Bake in the preheated oven for 15 minutes, until golden brown and slightly puffed. Cool on wire racks.

Cool the parkin on a wire rack. Wrap in foil and keep for at least a day before taking to the cricket match.

COFFEE AND CHOCOLATE CHIP SHORTBREADS

MAKES 24 BISCUITS

Homemade shortbread with a difference! The coffee stops the biscuits being too sweet, and the chocolate chips add a touch of luxury.

6oz (175g) unsalted butter or margarine	*2oz (60g) icing sugar, sieved*
6oz (175g) plain flour	*few drops vanilla essence*
1tbsp instant coffee granules	*2oz (60g) chocolate chips*

Cream the butter or margarine until soft then start to work in all the remaining ingredients except the chocolate chips. As the mixture begins to come together add the chocolate chips. Form the mixture into a roll about 15in (37.5cm) long, then cover the dough in plastic wrap and chill it for about 1 hour.

Preheat the oven to 180°C/350°F/Gas 4. Slice the dough into 24 pieces then flatten each piece slightly with a fork. Place the shortbreads on lightly greased baking sheets and bake for about 20–25 minutes. Cool for 5 minutes or so, to allow the biscuits to harden, then lift them onto a wire rack to cool completely.

POLLARD'S COTTAGE

Eric Pollard is, by nature, a solitary soul (when you get to know him you begin to understand why). I thought there was some salvation for him when he married Elizabeth Feldmann; alas, since her sad demise, he's gone from bad to worse. I didn't think he'd have anything to contribute when I mentioned the cookery book, but to my surprise he volunteered several of his favourites. It was also a surprise to me that he has time to cook. If you ask him, he'll call himself a market auctioneer, but that's only the tip of the iceberg: he also indulges in other nefarious activities. Most of them require him to be away from home on an evening!

As you can see, he has rather sophisticated tastes. After a long night out on the tiles in his bachelor days, he'd drop into a curry house for a meal, or pop into the local Italian restaurant on his way home. When Eric's cash supply dried up, as if often does, and he found it imposssible to extort money from any other source, he had no choice but to cook for himself at home – and that was the start of a love affair with food (his words, not mine). He used his favourite restaurants as inspiration, and went on from there. It sticks in my throat to compliment the man, but I must admit that the recipes he's chosen for me are perfect.

ERIC'S QUICK KORMA

SERVES 2

Marinading the meat for this mild curry gives it lots of flavour and also helps to cut down on the final cooking time. Not all curries take hours to cook.

3tbsp yogurt	*1tbsp oil*
juice of half a lemon	*1 small onion, finely*
2tsp curry paste	*sliced*
8oz (225g) lamb neck	*1tbsp ground almonds*
fillet, trimmed and	*salt and black pepper*
finely sliced	*1tbsp poppy seeds*

Mix together the yogurt, lemon juice and curry paste, add the meat and leave to marinade for at least 1 hour. Heat the oil in a pan and cook the onion until soft, then add the meat and marinade and cook quickly to brown on all sides. Reduce the heat, stir in the ground almonds and simmer for 20–30 minutes.

Season to taste with salt and pepper, then add the poppy seeds. Serve with chutney, rice and freshly cooked vegetables.

SUGAR-GLAZED STEAKS

SERVES 2

This was Elizabeth's favourite treat, and she passed it on to Eric.

2 fillet steaks, about 6oz	*2tsp demerara sugar*
(175g) each	*1 onion, chopped or*
1–2tbsp olive oil	*sliced*

Heat a frying-pan until very hot, then add one tablespoon of oil and the steaks and cook for 3–4 minutes on the first side. Turn the steaks and cook on the second side whilst preheating the grill. Transfer the steaks to the grill pan and top each one with a teaspoon of demerara. Grill until the sugar has melted. Cook the onions quickly in the frying-pan with the remaining olive oil until well browned, then serve the onions with the steak.

ERIC'S CHICKEN KIEV

SERVES 2

Preparing Chicken Kiev at home is quite fiddly and time-consuming. Buying it ready-prepared is such a give-away as it always looks the same. Eric has developed his own recipe which has all the flavour of the classic dish but does not require deep-frying. In fact, it is so tasty that he might even persuade you that his dish is the best! Cook the chicken over a moderate heat so that the butter does not brown too much.

2 boneless chicken	*1tbsp olive oil*
breasts, skinned	*1oz (30g) fresh white*
3oz (90g) prepared	*breadcrumbs*
garlic butter	

Carefully cut horizontally through the chicken breasts to make a pocket in each. Divide the garlic butter into three and place one piece in each chicken breast, then heat the remainder with the oil in a frying-pan. Add the chicken, smooth side down, and cook for 10 minutes over a medium heat, spooning a little of the butter over the breasts.

Turn the chicken, press the breadcrumbs onto the cooked surface and spoon a generous amount of the garlic butter over the crumbs. Cook for 10 minutes on the second side, then pierce the chicken with a sharp knife to check that it is cooked through. Serve with a tossed salad and fresh crusty bread.

CLAFOUTIS

SERVES 4

It's not that Eric actually entertains all that much but, when he does, this is the sort of pudding that appeals to him – a posh French name but it's really little more than a posh batter pudding!

14oz (400g) can pitted black cherries, drained and syrup reserved	³/4pt (430ml) milk 2tbsp brandy 1oz (30g) unsalted butter
3 eggs, size 3, beaten 1¹/2oz (45g) plain flour 3oz (90g) caster sugar	caster or icing sugar for decoration

Preheat the oven to 200°C/400°F/Gas 6. Lightly butter a suitable ovenproof dish and arrange the cherries in the bottom, reserving the juice to serve with the clafoutis. Whisk the eggs with the flour and sugar until smooth. Heat the milk until almost boiling, then pour it onto the egg mixture, whisking all the time. Pour the batter over the cherries, then drizzle the brandy over the top and dot with slivers of butter.

Bake in the preheated oven for 30 minutes, until set and lightly golden. Allow to cool then dredge with caster or icing sugar and serve warm. The cherry juice may be thickened with a teaspoon of arrowroot, if preferred.

CREAMY BROCCOLI SOUP

SERVES 3–4

Eric goes for anything that is showy and requires little effort. This soup is luxuriously different, but very easy to make.

It almost tastes like asparagus – another con!

1½oz (45g) butter
1 onion, finely sliced
1 large head of broccoli,
  weighing about 12oz
  (340g), chopped

1½pt (850ml) vegetable
  stock or water
salt and freshly ground
  black pepper
3–4tbsp double cream

Cook the onion slowly in the butter, then add the broccoli and stock or water. Bring to the boil then simmer for about 15 minutes, until the broccoli is tender. Cool slightly, then pour into a liquidiser or food processor and blend until smooth. Return the soup to the pan, season to taste and reheat if necessary. Add the cream just before serving.

PEPPER AND MOZZARELLA SALAD

SERVES 2

Eric loves roasted peppers but he certainly can't be bothered to do them himself. Instead he has devised a Mediterranean-style salad using canned pimentos, plenty of garlic and a good olive oil. Never serve this salad chilled – it will inhibit the flavours.

salad leaves
5oz (150g) mozzarella,
  drained and thinly
  sliced
14oz (400g) can
  pimentos, drained and
  sliced

1 large, ripe avocado,
  diced
1 clove garlic, finely
  sliced
3tbsp extra virgin olive
  oil
salt and black pepper

Place the salad leaves in the bottom of a serving dish or on individual plates and arrange the mozzarella over them. Mix the sliced pimentos with the avocado and garlic, add the olive oil then season lightly. Pile the mixture onto the cheese and serve immediately.

MEDITERRANEAN FISH STEW

SERVES 2–3

Eric has got very sophisticated tastes and certainly leans towards the finer things in life. However, he wouldn't spend time cleaning mussels and chopping up squid for this fish stew, although neither task takes very long. A bag of frozen seafood cocktail is his way of cheating with the preparation of this dish.

2tbsp olive oil
1 small bulb fennel,
  trimmed and finely

sliced (reserve feathery
  fronds for garnish)
¼pt (150ml)white wine

19oz (540g) jar tomato
  sauce base eg, Salsina
salt and black pepper

14oz (400g) packet
  frozen seafood cocktail

Heat the oil in a large pan, add the fennel and cook slowly until soft but not browned. Add the wine and boil until it is slightly reduced, then stir in the tomato sauce base. Season well and simmer for 5–10 minutes, until slightly thickened.

Add the seafood to the pan and return the mixture to the boil. Simmer for 5 minutes, then season again and serve, garnished with the fennel fronds.

BEEF CASSEROLE WITH PARSLEY DUMPLINGS

SERVES 4-6

Elizabeth used to make this for Eric; she added a few extras to a basic casserole recipe to make it just a little more special. Nowadays he sometimes serves this to his poker-playing cronies.

3tbsp oil
2 large onions, finely
  sliced
1½lb (680g) chuck or
  stewing steak, diced
1tbsp seasoned flour
1 clove garlic, crushed
2 large carrots, peeled

and thickly sliced
2 medium parsnips,
  peeled and thickly
  sliced
salt and freshly ground
  black pepper
bouquet garni
¾pt (440ml) bitter beer

FOR THE DUMPLINGS

4oz (120g) self-raising
  flour
2oz (60g) shredded suet

pinch of salt
1tbsp freshly chopped
  parsley

Preheat the oven to 160°C/325°F/Gas 3. Cook the onions in the oil until soft, then increase the heat. Toss the meat in the seasoned flour, then add it to the pan and brown on all sides. Add the garlic, carrots and parsnips with the seasonings, then pour in the beer. Bring to the boil, stirring from time to time, then cover the casserole and transfer it to the preheated oven for 2½ hours.

Prepare the dumplings towards the end of the cooking period. Mix together the flour, suet, salt and parsley, then add sufficient water to give a slightly soft but manageable dough. Knead lightly on a floured surface, then shape into 8 dumplings. Increase the oven temperature to 190°C/375°F/Gas 5. Season the beef to taste then drop the dumplings into the casserole, replace the lid and cook for a further 20–25 minutes, until the dumplings are puffed and cooked.

ORIENTAL PORK

SERVES 4

Pork fillet is always quick to cook and so is a real favourite with Eric. Marinade the meat for a minimum of 1 hour and a maximum of 6 – the flavour of this dish is absolutely delicious. He serves it with buttered noodles or tagliatelle.

1lb (460g) pork fillet in 1 or 2 pieces	*2tbsp hoi-sin sauce*
1 small piece root ginger	*2tbsp soy sauce*
2tbsp satay sauce	*1 clove garlic, crushed*

Trim the pork fillet of any fat and sinew. Grate the ginger coarsely, including the skin, then gather the shreds up in your hand. Squeeze all the juice from the ginger into a suitable dish, then discard the fibrous pulp. Add the sauces and garlic to the ginger juice and mix well. Turn the pork in the marinade until it is well coated then leave, covered, in the fridge for up to 6 hours, turning once or twice.

Preheat the oven to 200°C/400 °F/Gas 6. Place the meat and the marinade in a small roasting tin and cook for 40 minutes, basting occasionally. Allow the meat to stand for 5 minutes before slicing, and stir any remaining marinade into the cooked tagliatelle.

GRAPE BRULEE

SERVES 2

Real brûlées are made with a thick cream set with eggs. Eric cheats and uses a Greek-style yogurt. He also mixes crushed ginger nuts with the sugar topping for extra crunch – and to cut down the grilling time!

3–4oz (90–120g) seedless grapes, halved	*style set natural yogurt*
5oz (150g) tub Greek-	*2 ginger nut biscuits*
	2tbsp demerara sugar

Preheat the grill. Divide the grapes between two large ramekin dishes and top with a thick layer of the yogurt. Crush the biscuits in a bag by hitting them with a rolling pin, then mix in the sugar. Spoon the mixture in a thick layer over the yogurt, covering it completely, and grill until the sugar melts, in about one minute. Allow to cool, then chill until required.

HOME FARM

It was only after I left Home Farm that I actually started to appreciate the beauty and grandeur of the place. As you stroll down the tree-lined drive, the mullioned windows sparkle through the Virginia creeper. The well-kept lawn feels like velvet underfoot. I worked hard, played hard and took for granted the serenity around me – until it was too late.

The welcoming dining-room, with its beautiful French windows and impressive stone fireplace, has been the scene of numerous dinner parties over the years. Kim spent may long hours agonising over the decor of the house, for when the Tates bought Home Farm over six years ago, the historical building was suffering from neglect. Previous owners (and sadly that includes me) had found themselves unable to finance any restoration. Frank's fortune changed all that, and Home Farm has been returned to its former seventeenth-century splendour.

The long, dark wooden dining-table is in keeping with the grandeur of this impressive home. In days gone by, the squire dined with noblemen of the court who talked of the split with Rome, and the love life of their beloved Henry VIII. Now Squire Frank Tate courts businessmen and local politicians, and dinner talk is more about closing deals and profit margins. Nevertheless, visitors to Home Farm never fail to be impressed by its grace and beauty. Dinner there is always a memorable occasion.

SQUID GOULASH SOUP

SERVES 8

Do check that your guests all eat shellfish before you serve this delicious soup – Kim never tells them in advance that it is squid as some people think that they won't like it, but they always do! It is quite rich, so you don't need to serve very much to each person.

1tbsp extra virgin olive oil
1oz (30g) butter
1 medium onion, finely sliced
1 clove garlic, sliced or crushed
2tsp paprika

1lb (460g) squid tubes, cut into rings
17oz (500g) passata
1pt (570ml) fish or vegetable stock
salt and freshly ground black pepper

Heat the oil and butter together in a large pan, add the onion and garlic and cook until soft. Stir in the paprika and the prepared squid, turn up the heat a little and cook until the squid has stiffened. Add the passata, stock and a little seasoning, then bring the soup to the boil. Cover and simmer slowly for 1½ hours. Season to taste before serving.

NORMANDY PHEASANT

SERVES 8

Some recipes tell you that one pheasant will serve three people, but when you have as many birds as the Tates you can afford to be generous with the portions! Some recipes for Normandy Pheasant suggest cooking it just in butter, Calvados and cream – Kim has modified the recipe since Frank's illness to be slightly less rich, but still luxurious.

2 brace of pheasants
6 dessert apples, peeled and grated
3oz (90g) unsalted butter
salt and freshly ground black pepper

¼pt (150ml) Calvados
¾pt (440ml) dry cider
½pt (280ml) double cream
freshly chopped parsley to serve

Preheat the oven to 200°C/400°F/Gas 6. Joint the pheasants to make them easier to serve. Remove the legs and thighs in one piece. Trim off and discard the wings, or add them to the stock pot. Remove the breasts, keeping them on the bone if possible, but cutting through from the backbone at the wing. Use the backbones for stock.

Make a layer of the grated apples in the bottom of an ovenproof dish, preferably cast iron. Melt the butter in a large frying-pan and brown the pheasant pieces, a few at a time, on both sides. Do not attempt to turn them until they release readily, otherwise the presentation of the joints will be spoiled. Transfer the browned pheasant to the bed of apples and continue until all the pieces are browned. Season lightly with salt and pepper.

Heat the Calvados gently – this is easiest to do in a metal ladle. Flame the Calvados, pour it into the meat juices in the pan and leave until the flames subside. The pan should not be on the heat during this process. Place over a medium heat and cook, stirring constantly to scrape up any meat sediment from the bottom of the pan, until the liquid has reduced by about half. Add the cider and return the liquid to the boil, then pour it over the pheasant, cover and cook in the preheated oven for 30–40 minutes, until tender.

Transfer the pheasant to a warmed serving dish. Boil the sauce until well reduced, then stir in the cream and boil again. Season to taste and add a little sugar if necessary. Pour the sauce over the pheasant, garnish with freshly chopped parsley and serve.

POTATO & CELERIAC OLIVE OIL MASH

SERVES 8

Potatoes mashed with olive oil and garlic are a delicious vegetable dish – add some celeriac to the mix and you have a dinner party winner. This makes the perfect accompaniment to Kim's Normandy Pheasant, and the olive oil is a lot more healthy for Frank than loads of cream in the mash. You might choose to call this a purée if serving it at a dinner party!

1 celeriac weighing about 1¹/2lb (680g), peeled and chopped	*salt and freshly ground black pepper*
2¹/2lb (1.15kg) potatoes, peeled and chopped	*6tbsp extra virgin olive oil*
	1–2 cloves garlic

Preheat the oven to 200°C/400°F/Gas 6. Lightly butter a gratin dish. Chop the celeriac and potatoes into evenly-sized pieces and cook them together in boiling salted water for 20 minutes, or until soft. Drain thoroughly, then return them to the pan over the heat for just a few seconds, to dry off any water.

Mash the vegetables with the seasonings, oil and as much freshly crushed garlic as you consider to be socially acceptable! Pile the mash into the gratin dish and bake in the hot oven for about 30 minutes, until browned and slightly crispy on top. Serve hot – any left-overs make delicious rissoles.

HOME FARM PROFITEROLES

SERVES 8

Kim has found that, no matter how long she spends thumbing through her recipe books for new ideas, profiteroles are always a favourite with her guests. She always makes them quite large, so that they appear to be even more of a treat, and prepares a rich chocolate sauce to serve with them. Profiteroles really are not difficult things to make – homemade and shop-bought simply do not compare. Kim usually serves fresh fruit as a healthy alternative for Frank to this rich dessert.

FOR THE PASTRY

3oz (90g) butter	*12tbsp plain flour*
8fl oz (225ml) water	*3 eggs, size 3, beaten*

FOR THE SAUCE

7oz (200g) bar plain chocolate	*1tsp coffee essence*
1oz (30g) butter	*¹/2pt (280ml) crème fraîche*
3tbsp clear honey	

FOR THE FILLING

³/4pt (430ml) double cream, whipped	*8–12oz (225–340g) soft fruits in season*

Preheat the oven to 210°C/425°F/Gas 7, and lightly butter two baking sheets. Heat the butter and water together until the butter has melted, then bring to the boil – the liquid should be boiling rapidly. Shoot the sieved flour into the pan, remove it instantly from the heat and beat the mixture vigorously until it leaves the sides of the pan and forms a ball. (Once the flour is well mixed into the liquid, the mixture may be transferred to a food mixer for beating.) Gradually beat in the eggs until the pastry is very smooth and shiny, and is the correct consistency to pipe.

Pipe or spoon the mixture onto the baking sheets – Kim uses two dessert spoons to shape generously sized profiteroles. Bake them in the preheated oven for 30 minutes, then reduce the temperature to 180°C/350°F/Gas 4. Slit the pastries with a sharp knife then return them to the oven for a further 15–20 minutes, until crisp and dry inside. Transfer to a wire rack to cool.

Melt all the ingredients for the sauce, except the crème fraîche, together in a bowl over a pan of water. Remove from the heat and cool slightly, then beat in the crème. Allow to cool.

Fill the profiteroles with whipped cream and fresh soft fruits, then pile them into a serving dish – you can scatter some fruits over the choux buns in the bowl if you wish. Pour the sauce over the profiteroles before serving.

Before his heart attack Frank paid little attention to his diet. He worked long hours, didn't eat at regular times, and was permanently stressed…he was a disaster waiting to happen. Kim felt guilty after the event; perhaps she should have seen what was coming. It's easy to apportion blame in retrospect, but really it's the aftercare that's important. Since making his recovery Frank has determined to change his lifestyle. Kim and Christopher share some of the burdens of the business, and Kim has worked out a new diet for Frank, based on a nutritionist's advice and her own researches into healthy eating. She's been astonishingly successful so far in improving the quality of his life. Frank, who started work as a haulage driver who existed on a diet of fried egg, chips, steak and sausages, was no easy convert to the healthy alternative of low-fat foods, beans, pasta and pulses. Thanks to Kim's expertise there's no turning back now.

WATERCRESS-STUFFED MUSHROOMS

SERVES 4 AS A STARTER, OR 2 AS A LIGHT MEAL

Field mushrooms are plentiful around Home Farm in the autumn. They make a flavour-packed natural basket for a topping of cottage cheese and watercress – Frank never thought he would enjoy cottage cheese! Large cultivated mushrooms may be used when field mushrooms are not available.

4 field mushrooms, peeled and trimmed
freshly ground black pepper
olive oil
8oz (225g) low fat cottage cheese
2 spring onions, finely chopped

1 bunch watercress, trimmed and very finely chopped
freshly cooked toast to serve
tomato to garnish (optional)

Season the mushrooms lightly with freshly ground black pepper and brush them with a little olive oil. Grill the mushrooms under a medium heat for 3–4 minutes until just tender.

Mix together the cottage cheese, spring onions and watercress. Season with pepper then pile the mixture into the mushrooms. Grill for a further 4–5 minutes, until warmed through. Serve on hot toast, garnished with tomato.

SMOKED HADDOCK LASAGNE

SERVES 6

Pasta is a low fat food – it's the sauces that are served with it that pile on the calories and the cholesterol! This lasagne is full of flavour and ideal for Frank's diet. If he hasn't had many eggs during the week, then Kim will add a couple of hard boiled eggs with the fish, for a little extra flavour. Kim prefers to use fresh pasta that she par-boils for this dish: it has a better flavour than the convenient no-cook variety, and the completed lasagne requires less cooking time in the Aga when fresh pasta is used.

1lb (460g) smoked haddock fillets
½pt (280ml) water
1–1¼lb (460–570g) prepared mixed vegetables, carrots, courgettes, parsnips, onions, leeks etc
14oz (400g) can chopped tomatoes
freshly ground black pepper

2 hard-boiled eggs, peeled and chopped (optional)
6–8 sheets lasagne (use a dough mix of 4oz (120g) flour and 1 egg for homemade pasta)
17oz (500g) low fat fromage frais
1½oz (45g) grated Parmesan cheese (optional)

Poach the smoked haddock in the water for about 5 minutes, until just cooked. Add the water to the prepared vegetables and tomatoes in a pan and cook for 20–25 minutes, until the vegetables are just tender and the sauce has reduced. Season to taste with pepper. Skin and flake the fish.

Cook the lasagne in plenty of boiling water for 2–3 minutes, or as directed. Drain and lay out on clean cloths until required – this prevents the pasta sheets from sticking together.

Preheat the oven to 220°C/425°F/Gas 7. Place half the vegetable mixture in the bottom of an ovenproof dish and cover with half the lasagne. Top with the smoked haddock and the chopped hard boiled eggs, then add the remaining vegetables and lasagne.

Beat the fromage frais with the Parmesan cheese and a little black pepper, then spread the mixture over the lasagne. Bake in the preheated oven for 20 minutes, until lightly browned. Serve with freshly cooked green vegetables or a salad.

Dinner parties for Kim's hunting friends tend to be fraught affairs, so the food has to be especially good to compensate. Frank isn't a fan of hunting, and takes quite a negative view of it. Of course, he wouldn't stand in the way of Kim's interests; he just doesn't put himself out for them. The delicious recipes that follow manage to cheer up her husband and placate her dinner-party guests for her husband's frequent rudeness. It's amazing how much people are prepared to excuse when they're tempted by a wonderful meal!

HOME FARM STIRRUP CUP

SERVES 12

When Kim first gave a lawn meet at Home Farm she was anxious that everything should be just right and go smoothly. The biggest problem was finding a tra-ditional recipe for stirrup cup, to serve to the horse-men before they left – she couldn't find one any-where! Rather than admit defeat and just serve sher-ry, Kim devised this recipe for a hot red wine and brandy cup.

1 bottle full-bodied red wine	*1pt (570ml) water*
4oz (120g) demerara sugar	*¼pt (150ml) orange curaçao*
3 cinnamon sticks, broken in half	*¼pt (150ml) brandy orange slices for serving*

Heat the wine, sugar, cinnamon and water together until almost boiling, then remove the pan from the heat and stir to ensure that the sugar has completely dissolved.

Add the remaining ingredients, with the oranges sliced and then cut into small triangular segments. Serve immediately.

HORSEBACK SAVOURIES

MAKES 12

After a hunt everyone has very healthy appetites so Kim always produces a filling, satisfying and traditional meal. She ends with savoury toasts topped with rarebit mixture and a devil-on-horseback – a prune wrapped in bacon.

6 rashers streaky bacon, rinded and stretched	good pinch of dry mustard
12 small prunes, pitted	salt and freshly ground black pepper
4oz (120g) Wensleydale or Cheddar cheese, crumbled or grated	2tbsp bitter beer
1oz (30g) butter	3 slices fresh toast, crusts cut off and quartered

Preheat the oven to 200°C/400°F/Gas 6. Prepare the horseback garnish by stretching the bacon rashers and cutting them in two. Wrap a prune in each piece of bacon, then bake in the preheated oven for 5–10 minutes while preparing the savoury.

Place all the remaining ingredients in a small pan and heat together until melted and creamy. Spread the mixture onto the toast quarters and grill until the cheese is lightly browned. Top each savoury with a devil on horseback before serving.

BEEF CHASSEUR

SERVES 4

This is Kim's version of the classic French dish – hunter's beef. There is so much to do to prepare for the hunt that Kim has to choose a recipe for dinner that is rich, delicious and warming, but which will look after itself, improving with a long slow cooking period. This is a very easy dish to prepare, but cooked in brandy and red wine, the beef is bound to impress the Hunt Master.

4 large slices braising steak, each weighing about 8oz (225g)	3fl oz (90ml) brandy
1tbsp seasoned flour	¹/2pt (280ml) full-bodied red wine
1oz (30g) butter	salt and freshly ground black pepper
3tbsp fruity olive oil	3–4 sprigs fresh thyme
4 rashers streaky bacon, rinded and diced	3 bay leaves
2 large onions, finely sliced	14oz (400g) can chopped tomatoes with herbs
1–2 cloves garlic, crushed	8oz (225g) button mushrooms, sliced

Preheat the oven to 160°C/325°F/Gas 3. Toss the beef in the seasoned flour whilst heating the butter and olive oil together in a large flameproof casserole. Add the beef and brown thoroughly on both sides, then remove the beef from the pan and leave it on a plate.

Add the bacon, onions and garlic to the pan and cook until well browned – browning the onions will add extra richness to the finished dish. Heat the brandy, then pour it into the pan and ignite it. Turn off the heat and wait for the flames to subside. Immediately stir up any sediment from the bottom of the casserole – it will come away after being loosened by the brandy.

Return the casserole to the heat and gradually add the red wine. Return the beef to the pan and add the seasonings and the tomatoes. Bring the casserole to the boil, then cover and cook slowly in the preheated oven for 2 hours.

Slice the mushrooms and stir them into the beef – add a little more wine if necessary. Cover and cook for a further 30 minutes, then season before serving. Beef chasseur will not spoil if it is cooked for an hour or so longer, but do turn the oven down or keep the wine in the sauce topped up, to prevent it from cooking dry.

Home Farm Estate borders the Holiday Village, and it's wonderful during the long summer months when the evening air is filled with the aroma of barbecued food. These recipes are ideal for those blissful summer evenings when the red sun is in the western sky, the swallows and martins flit lightly overhead and the golden corn is almost ready for harvest.

HERBY CHEESEBURGERS

SERVES 4

Beefburgers are one of the most popular of barbecue foods but, once you have tasted these, you'll never be happy with shop-bought burgers again!

1lb (460g) lean minced beef	1tbsp freshly chopped mixed herbs
4oz (120g) wholewheat breadcrumbs	salt and black pepper
1 small onion, very finely chopped	3oz (90g) blue cheese, finely crumbled
	1 egg, size 3, beaten

Mix all the ingredients together, binding them with the beaten egg. It is important that the onion is very finely chopped or the beefburgers will break up during cooking. Form the mixture into 4 burgers, shaping them with floured hands. Chill until required.

Cook the beefburgers for about 10 minutes on each side – they need longer to cook than shop burgers as they are so much thicker.

SPICED LAMB KOFTAS

SERVES 6, MAKES 24 KOFTAS

An Indian idea that is ideal for the barbecue – these spicy mouthfuls of lamb are similar to a meatball mix but are shaped around skewers to make them easier to cook over the coals.

1lb (460g) minced lamb	*1 clove garlic*
4oz (120g) white	*1 green chilli, cored and*
breadcrumbs	*seeded*
1¹/₂oz (45g) desiccated	*¹/₂tsp salt*
coconut	*1 egg, size 3, beaten*
1 small onion	*1tbsp curry paste*

Mix the lamb, breadcrumbs and coconut together in a bowl. Place the onion, garlic and chilli in a liquidiser or food processor and chop until very fine and almost liquid. Add the vegetables to the meat with the salt and mix well.

Beat the egg with the curry paste, then pour into the lamb mixture to bind the meat together. Form

small spoonfuls of mixture into little sausage shapes around metal skewers – fit 4–6 onto each skewer.

Cook the koftas for about 10–15 minutes, turning once during cooking. Serve with a yogurt and cucumber dip.

PEPPER AND KIDNEY KEBABS

SERVES 4

The barbecue is the perfect way of cooking kebabs – the vegetables take on a marvellous char-grilled appearance, slightly blackened, which all adds extra colour and flavour to the finished dish.

8 lamb's kidneys, cored	*2tbsp smooth Dijon*
and trimmed	*mustard*
2 small green peppers,	*2tbsp red wine*
cored and seeded	*salt and freshly ground*
4 small shallots	*black pepper*

Cut the kidneys in two and cut the peppers into squares of about 1in (2.5cm). Thread the kidneys and peppers alternately onto 4 barbecue skewers then finish each with a shallot.

Mix the mustard, wine and seasonings together and use to baste the kebabs. Cook on the barbecue for 10–15 minutes, turning and basting from time to time.

HOME FARM NURSERY

It took Nick Bates a long time to realise that he could save some money by using fresh produce from the gardens at Home Farm. Dinner for him meant a cold pie or a sandwich and tea was fish and chips from the mobile chippy. When he moved to the nursery at Home Farm, Kim said he could help himself to the fruit and vegetables. Caroline Bates, ever practical (and a wonderful woman) gave him some useful recipes – his favourite is the Artichoke and Lemon Soup. He finds the fact that most of the food he cooks for himself and for his young daughter has been watered and grown by his own hands very rewarding. He'll argue that it makes the food taste even better. Perhaps he's right – who knows.

ARTICHOKE AND LEMON SOUP

SERVES 6

As Nick well knows, once you have Jerusalem artichokes in your garden or allotment, you have them almost for life, so it is as well to have a few good recipes ready to use them up! This soup is rich and buttery with a refreshing tang of lemon. Wash the artichokes thoroughly and then there is no need to peel them, which is a very fiddly job.

2oz (60g) butter	2pt (1.14l) vegetable
1 large onion, finely	stock
sliced	salt and black pepper
1 1/2lb (680g) Jerusalem	nutmeg to taste
artichokes, scrubbed	3 lemons, grated rind
and roughly chopped	and juice

Melt the butter in a large saucepan, add the onion and cook slowly until soft – do not allow the butter or onions to brown or the final flavour of the soup will be spoiled. Add the artichokes and stock, then stir in some seasonings and nutmeg to taste. Add the grated lemon rind then bring the soup to the boil and simmer, covered, for 30 minutes.

Allow the soup to cool for a few minutes before transferring to a liquidiser or food processor and blending until smooth. Add the lemon juice to the soup, then reheat gently and season to taste. Do not allow the soup to boil once you have added the lemon juice. Serve with fresh crusty bread.

CARAMELISED ONION TART

SERVES 4–6

Onions are an essential part of so many recipes yet they are seldom allowed to revel in their own glory. All you need for this recipe is time – it is quite cheap to prepare but to get the best possible flavour from the onions they require a long, slow cooking.

FOR THE FILLING

1 1/2lb (680g) onions,	2 bay leaves
finely sliced	4 small cloves garlic,
3tbsp fruity olive oil	peeled but left whole
freshly ground black	2oz (50g) can anchovy
pepper	fillets in olive oil
1tbsp freshly chopped	
thyme, or 1tsp dried	

FOR THE BASE

8oz (225g) plain flour	1 egg, size 3, beaten
1/2tsp salt	6tbsp fruity olive oil
1oz (30g) almonds,	
toasted and chopped	

Cook the onions in the oil until just starting to brown, then add the seasonings and garlic, cover the pan and reduce the heat. Stew slowly for at least 1 hour.

Prepare the base. Mix the flour, salt and chopped almonds together, then add the egg and oil. Mix to a firm but manageable dough, adding 1–2tbsp of water if necessary. Turn onto a lightly floured surface and knead gently into a smooth ball.

Roll out the dough and use to line a 9in (22.5cm) sandwich tin. It is easiest to roll the dough on some non-stick baking parchment – reshape the dough during rolling to keep it circular. This is more like a dough than a pastry so you can press it into shape in the tin. Chill for at least 45 minutes, while the onions are cooking.

Preheat the oven to 220°C/425°F/Gas 7. Spoon the onion mixture into the tart case, removing the bay leaves, and top with the anchovy fillets, pouring the oil from the can over the tart. Bake the tart for 25 minutes, until the base is a pale golden brown. Cool slightly, then serve the tart warm.

GOOSEBERRY CURD CHEESECAKE

SERVES 6–8

The slightly acid flavour of gooseberries cuts through the deliciously tooth-encasing texture of a baked cheesecake to make a fruity cheesecake which is not too rich. Elderflower cordial is on sale at the Heritage Farm Shop.

FOR THE BASE

8oz (225g) digestive biscuits, crushed
1tsp ground mixed spice

1oz (30g) caster sugar
4oz (120g) butter, melted

FOR THE FILLING

12oz (340g) prepared gooseberries
2tbsp elderflower cordial
8oz (225g) curd cheese
3oz (90g) caster sugar

2oz (60g) plain flour
7fl oz (200ml) crème fraîche
3 eggs, size 3, beaten

Preheat the oven to 160°C/325°F/Gas 3. Prepare the biscuit base by mixing all the ingredients together, then press the buttered crumbs onto the base and sides of a deep 8in (20cm) flan tin with a loose bottom. Smooth over the crumbs, then chill the base until required.

Stew the gooseberries with the elderflower cordial and as little water as possible until soft. Transfer to a liquidiser or food processor and blend until smooth.

Beat the curd cheese in a large bowl until soft. Add the sugar, flour and crème fraîche then beat in the eggs, one by one. Continue beating until smooth, then stir in the gooseberry purée. Pour the filling into the biscuit base then bake in the pre-heated oven for 1 hour, until set. Leave to cool in the oven with the door open for 30 minutes. Allow the cheesecake to cool at room temperature then chill in the 'fridge for about 2 hours before serving.

Nick has been Frank Tate's gardener up at Home Farm for several years now. He found the job rather tedious in the early days when the vegetable garden only produced cabbages, sprouts and potatoes. Thankfully Frank was open to new ideas, and now the vegetable garden is the envy of North Yorkshire. Artichokes, broccoli, spinach and a wide variety of herbs are just a few of the new lines Nick has introduced.

There was a time when Nick thought he might have to give up gardening to move to Leeds to be nearer his daughter when his relationship with Elsa broke down. He never had to make that sacrifice as Elsa decided to return Alice to her rightful place – Emmerdale. Alice is proud of her father; he isn't just the best gardener in all the world, he's also known for his prize marrows. He knocked the (then) reigning marrow king – Amos Brearly – off his throne a few years ago. Since then, Nick has never looked back. His recipes are quite straightforward and simple and, as you'd imagine, vegetables form the main ingredients.

ITALIAN SPINACH SALAD

SERVES 2

Once the perpetual spinach is growing well there is plenty for cooking and for eating raw in salads. Choose small, young leaves and wash them thoroughly. This salad is delicious.

1 clove garlic
3–4oz (90–120g) young spinach leaves
2 ripe tomatoes, cut into segments
4 halves sun-dried tomatoes in oil, drained and shredded
3oz (90g) Dolcelatte cheese, finely chopped
4 large leaves fresh basil, roughly torn
croûtons
3–4tbsp vinaigrette dressing

Cut the garlic in half and rub it around the inside of a salad bowl, then discard the clove. Place the spinach in the bowl and add all the remaining ingredients. Toss together with the vinaigrette. Serve the salad immediately, at room temperature – this helps to accentuate the flavours.

PEPPER, PESTO AND PINE NUT PASTA

SERVES 3

Home Farm Nursery has moved into peppers with great success. This pasta recipe has a real flavour of Italy about it, especially when made with a good pesto sauce. Add a few leaves of fresh basil, torn into small pieces, if you have any to hand.

3tbsp olive oil
2 red peppers, seeded and chopped
1 yellow pepper, seeded and chopped
1–2 cloves garlic, sliced
3tbsp pesto sauce
1oz (30g) pine kernels
salt and freshly ground black pepper
8oz (225g) spaghetti, cooked in boiling water
grated Parmesan

Heat the oil in a frying-pan, add the peppers and cook quickly for 5–6 minutes, until soft but still bright in colour. Add the garlic then transfer to a liquidiser or food processor and blend until smooth. Return the pepper mixture to the pan and heat for 2–3 minutes to drive off any surplus water.

Stir the pesto and pine nuts into the pepper mixture, season if necessary. Add the drained, cooked spaghetti and toss until coated in the sauce. Serve on warm plates, topped with Parmesan cheese.

LIME & RHUBARB MOUSSE

SERVES 6

Rhubarb is one of the first spring fruits and forced young stems have the most delicious flavour. It combines well with limes and together they make a refreshing, light mousse.

1½lb (680g) young forced rhubarb, trimmed and chopped
7fl oz (200ml) water
4oz (120g) caster sugar, or to taste
3 limes, grated rind and juice
½oz (15g) powdered gelatine
½pt (280ml) whipping cream

Stew the rhubarb with the water and sugar until the rhubarb is just soft, then add the grated lime rind. Pour into a liquidiser or food processor and blend until smooth.

Heat the lime juice then add the gelatine and stir well. Leave for 1–2 minutes until dissolved and stir again. Add the gelatine mixture to the rhubarb. Chill until just beginning to set.

Whip the cream until thick and floppy but not stiff. Fold into the rhubarb then turn the mixture into a suitable soufflé dish or glass bowl. Chill for about 2 hours, until set.

HERITAGE FARM SHOP

The Heritage Farm Shop was actually Sarah Sugden's idea. Long ago, Kathy Tate, Dolly Skilbeck and Annie Sugden opened a small shop at Emmerdale Farm selling farm produce, jams, pickles and cheeses. It had long since disappeared when Sarah arrived on the scene, but she liked the notion of running a shop dedicated to local produce. When Jack told her about the Emmerdale Shop, she was determined to resurrect something similar. Frank Tate was an ideal partner, and so the Heritage Farm Shop was

born. Visitors have been really impressed by the various pickles and chutneys, jams and marmalades, which are made from the old recipes passed down by word of mouth to successive generations of farmer's wives. Annie Sugden taught Sarah how to pickle onions, Jan Glover's mother passed on her Orange and Whisky Marmalade recipe to her daughter.

Now *you* can be part of that tradition, too, as I in turn hand these traditional Emmerdale family recipes over to you.

SPICED PEAR CHUTNEY

MAKES ABOUT 4LB (1.8KG)

This unusual chutney is popular at the Heritage Farm Shop. It is slightly sweet and needs to be left for 2–3 months before eating, to allow the flavours to develop.

8oz (225g) onions, finely chopped	4oz (120g) seedless raisins
8oz (225g) celery, trimmed and finely chopped	1tsp salt
	1tsp ground ginger
	1tsp paprika
8oz (225g) ripe red tomatoes, chopped	1tsp cloves
2lb (900g) conference pears, peeled, cored and chopped	1½pt (850ml) distilled malt vinegar
	12oz (340g) demerara sugar

Place all the ingredients except the sugar in a preserving pan. Bring to the boil then simmer for 30 minutes, until the vegetables are soft and the liquid has reduced.

Add the sugar and stir until dissolved. Simmer for a further 35–40 minutes until thick. Cool the chutney slightly, then pot into warm jars, seal and label.

RED HOT CHUTNEY

MAKES ABOUT 4LB (1.8KG)

A highly spiced red tomato chutney that will add fire to cold meats and cheeses. It is also great for serving with barbecued chops and burgers – use it for bast-

ing and dipping too. Skin the tomatoes if you wish, but it is not necessary to do so.

4lb (1.8kg) red tomatoes, chopped	1tbsp salt
3 large fresh red chillis, seeded and finely chopped	1lb (460g) onions, finely chopped
1tbsp dried red chillis	1pt (570ml) distilled malt vinegar
1tsp cayenne pepper	12oz (340g) demerara sugar
2tsp paprika	

Place all the ingredients except the sugar in a large preserving pan, bring to the boil and then simmer for about 1 hour, until the onions are soft and the mixture is well reduced and thickened in the pan.

Stir in the sugar and return the chutney to the boil. Cook for a further 20–30 minutes or until the chutney is thick, then pour into warm jars and seal and label. Store for 1–2 months before using.

GARDENER'S CHUTNEY

MAKES ABOUT 10LB (4.6KG)

It is essential for anyone who enjoys growing their own vegetables to have a good recipe for green tomato chutney – when you live as far north as Emmerdale there are always green tomatoes left on the plants when the first frosts come. This chutney, which is always quite liquid, is wonderfully spiced and very tasty. An excellent chutney to serve with cold meats and baked potatoes.

6lb (2.7kg) green
tomatoes, washed and
chopped
3lb (1.4kg) onions, finely
chopped
2lb (900g) cooking
apples, peeled, cored
and chopped
1tsp ground mace

1tsp cloves
1¹/2tsp ground white
pepper
2oz (60g) white mustard
seeds
2oz (60g) coriander
seeds, lightly crushed
1¹/2tsp cayenne pepper
4oz (120g) salt

1¹/2pt (850ml) distilled
malt vinegar

3lb (1.4kg) demerara
sugar

Place all the ingredients except the sugar in a large preserving pan and stew for at least 1 hour, until the onions are soft and the liquid has reduced leaving a thick pulp. Add the sugar and stir until dissolved. Boil the chutney until it has thickened slightly, then pour into warm jars, seal and label.

SUNRISE MARMALADE

MAKES ABOUT 3LB (1.4KG)

This marmalade is made by stewing the fruit and then draining the pulp through a jelly bag. The zests of the fruit are blanched in boiling water before being added to the almost set jelly. You will need a zester to make this marmalade, a useful gadget to have in the kitchen.

3 grapefruit, weighing about 2lb (900g)	*1pt (570ml) boiling water*
5 lemons, weighing about 1lb (460g)	*3pt (1.7l) cold water*
	2lb (900g) granulated sugar

Wash the fruit and remove the zests from them, placing them in a small bowl. Pour the boiling water onto the zest and leave until required.

Chop the fruit and place it in a preserving pan with the cold water and bring to the boil. Simmer for about 1 hour, until reduced by half then turn the mixture into a jelly bag and allow it to drain into a bowl – do not squeeze the bag or the jelly will be cloudy.

Measure the liquid and make it up to 2pt (1.1l) with the water from the zest. Return the liquid to the preserving pan and add the sugar. Bring slowly to the boil, stirring to dissolve the sugar and then boil until setting point is reached. Allow the marmalade to cool for 20–30 minutes in the pan until starting to set.

Drain the zest of any remaining water, then stir it into the setting marmalade. Pour into warmed jars, then seal and label.

ORANGE AND WHISKY MARMALADE

MAKES ABOUT 9LB (4KG)

Orange marmalades are always the best sellers at the Heritage Farm. This recipe has a little whisky in it and is a great favourite with the men. As soon as the Seville oranges arrive in January large quantities of this marmalade are made, ready for the season.

3lb (1.4kg) Seville oranges, washed	*$\frac{1}{4}$pt (150ml) whisky*
juice of 2 lemons	*6lb (2.7kg) granulated sugar*
$5\frac{3}{4}$pt (3.25l) water	

Wash the oranges and squeeze the juice from them into a preserving pan. Scoop out the pith from the fruit shells – this is easiest to do with a teaspoon – and wrap it with any pips in muslin, tying it up into a bag. Chop the peel quite finely and add it to the pan with the muslin bag, water and whisky. Leave to stand for 6 hours or overnight.

Boil the fruit and then simmer for about 1½ hours, until the peel is soft and the liquid has reduced by about half. Remove the muslin bag, carefully squeezing out as much juice as possible.

Add the sugar and stir over a low heat until dissolved. Bring the marmalade to the boil and cook until setting point is reached. Take the pan from the heat and allow the marmalade to stand for 20 minutes before pouring into warm jars. If you pot the marmalade when too hot all the peel will float to the top of the jars. Seal and label the jars.

ALL-YEAR APRICOT JAM

MAKES ABOUT 5LB (2.3KG)

Fresh apricots have such a short season and appear right in the middle of the busiest time of year at the Heritage Farm. The home-made apricot jam is therefore made with dried apricots (which many people think have a better flavour anyway) so it can be made at any time of year in a quiet moment. The green of the pistachio kernels contrasts strikingly with the apricot orange of the jam.

1lb (460g) dried apricots, roughly chopped	3lb (1.4kg) granulated sugar
3pt (1.7l) water	1½oz (45g) pistachio kernels, roughly chopped
juice of 2 lemons	

Place the apricots, water and lemon juice in a preserving pan and soak for 6–8 hours.

Bring to the boil, then simmer the mixture for about 30 minutes, until the apricots are soft. Add the sugar and continue stirring until it is dissolved. Boil the jam until setting point is reached – stir carefully from time to time as this dried fruit is more likely to stick in the pan then fresh fruit.

Stand the jam for 20 minutes then stir in the pistachios. Pour into warm jars then seal and label.

ORCHARD JELLY

MAKES ABOUT 10LB (4.6KG)

The autumn is always so busy that there is seldom enough time to make preserves that require lots of peeling and chopping. This is therefore an ideal autumn jelly recipe – a well-coloured preserve with lots of flavour.

Don't be tempted to squeeze the jelly bag – this will make the resulting preserve cloudy.

6lb (2.7kg) cooking apples	4pt (2.3l) water
3lb (1.4kg) red plums	approx 5lb (2.3kg) sugar

Wash all the fruit. Chop the apples roughly, removing any bad bruises and pests if you are using windfalls. Remove any stalks from the plums and place all the fruit and the water in a large preserving pan. Cook slowly for about 1 hour, until the fruit is all reduced to a pulp. Pour the mixture into a jelly bag and leave it to drain overnight.

Measure the liquid and return it to the preserving pan with 1lb (460g) sugar to every 1pt (570ml). Bring slowly to the boil, stirring to dissolve the sugar, and then continue to boil until a gel or setting point is reached.

Skim any frothy scum from the top of the pan, then pour into warm jars and seal and label.

RHUBARB AND ORANGE PRESERVE

MAKES ABOUT 5LB (2.3KG)

This is a wonderful spring jam, although it is often made in the summer at the Heritage Farm to use up any rhubarb that is becoming too thick and tough for use in desserts. It is a great favourite in the shop with the visitors – it's just that little bit different. Yorkshire rhubarb is thought to be the best in England.

6 large sweet oranges	3lb (1.4kg) granulated sugar (approx)
2½lb (1.15kg) rhubarb, trimmed and finely sliced	

Wash the oranges and pare the zest from them – this is easiest done with a zester. Squeeze the juice from the oranges, and place it in a preserving pan with the zest and any flesh that comes from the oranges. Add the rhubarb and cook the fruits together gently until soft.

Weigh the fruit pulp then return it to the pan with 1lb (460g) sugar to every 1lb (460g) of pulp. Stir over a low heat until the sugar is dissolved, then bring to the boil and cook until the jam reaches setting point. Pour into warmed jars then seal and label.

Hotten Tasty

Home Farm, with its sprawling drive, oak doors and stone archway, is an impressive sight. At first glance it would seem that nothing has changed since the Verney family built it in the late 1600s. But appearances can be deceptive and in this case they most certainly are for, apart from the exterior, there is nothing ancient about this country seat. Since moving into the area five years ago, the nouveaux riches Tates have spent a fortune dragging the interior into the nineties. The sedate, historic aristocratic Verneys were replaced by a loud brash family who have played out their sagas, trials and tribulations on a public platform; rarely does a day go by without a mention of what the Tates have been up to. Life at Home Farm is never dull, but I must say I'm glad I don't live there. Somehow I don't think wealth has brought them much in the way of happiness. While I like Frank and Kim and don't hesitate to call them friends, I'm aware that people who have been sucked in by their glamorous lifestyle have often come away injured.

People like Kathy Tate. We were all so pleased for Kathy when she found happiness for a second time with Christopher Tate. The tragic death of her first husband Jackie in a shooting accident had affected us all. She deserved some good fortune, but sadly it wasn't to last. Christopher stormed into The Woolpack wine bar one evening and accused her in a very ungentlemanly manner of having an affair with Josh Lewis, my American wine merchant. As far as I knew it was all an invention of Christopher's imagination. Besides, she stayed with him when he sustained those terrible injuries in the air crash – and how did he repay her? By having an affair with Rachel. Poor Kathy. One inevitably looks at the parents, though; Frank's behaviour has hardly been exemplary. It was rumoured that he met Kim before his first wife died and the events surrounding his wife's death were somewhat suspicious! Kim's affair with the Master of the hunt, Neil Kincaid,

became public when Frank threw her out of Home Farm and gave Kincaid a thrashing at the hunt.

Still, the past is the past and life for the family seems to have settled back to normal. Frank and Kim re-married last Christmas and looked a picture of happiness. Frank has mellowed since his heart attack – I think it's made him realise there's more to life than success in business. After all, you can't take it with you.

Zoe, Frank's daughter, has been his constant support through good times and bad. I have enormous respect for that young woman. She has a very sensible head on her shoulders. She hasn't escaped the vicious tongues of the gossip-mongers, and they've said some extremely cruel things about her. In my experience she's always conducted herself with dignity. I'm reminded of a quiet afternoon in The Woolpack not that long ago. Christopher and Zoe were enjoying a pleasant lunch together when the peace was shattered by the entrance of a shrieking harridan. She accused Zoe of stealing her husband away from her. (This rather took us by surprise considering the rumours about Zoe that were flying round at the time.) Zoe conducted herself with supreme grace; she ignored the silly woman and discreetly left the pub. What more can a landlord ask of his clientèle?!

THE WINDSORS' POST OFFICE

Viv Windsor told me she wasn't a brilliant cook. She didn't have much time for it, and could never be bothered with recipe books. When I asked her to provide me with a selection of her favourite recipes she advised me not to waste my time. However, I persisted…and as it turned out I was quite right to do so.

Viv is a woman with a busy life. She has three children and a rather unruly husband to look after, as well as her full-time career as co-owner of the village post office. Understandably she likes to stay in the kitchen for the shortest possible time. Her recipes therefore are useful and easy-to-follow, and she knows how to take short cuts in the preparation of certain foods. She also knows how to make a simple dish special and appetising. Mealtimes are fun for the children thanks to Viv's imagination and flair – and even Vic admires her cooking!

VIV'S SWEET AND SOUR PORK

SERVES 4–6

Who can blame Viv for making use of the stock in the Post Office when it comes to producing satisfying meals for the family in between customers? This is a good way of using up left-over pork from a weekend roast, and you can add extra vegetables if you wish. Viv serves the pork with thread egg noodles which only have to stand in boiling water for a few minutes before serving – serve with rice if you prefer.

3tbsp oil	*14oz (390g) can sweet*
1 large onion, sliced	*and sour sauce, or a*
1lb (460g) cooked pork	*similar sized jar*
2 peppers, 1 red, 1 green,	*1–2tsp white wine*
cut into large dice	*vinegar*
8oz (227g) can	*salt to taste*
pineapple chunks	

Preheat the oven to 350F/180°C/Gas 4. Cook the onions in the oil in a large pan until just starting to soften, then add the pork and cook quickly until it is heated through and starting to brown all over. Stir in the peppers, the pineapple chunks and their juice and the sauce, mixing well to ensure that the meat is coated in the sauce.

Bring to the boil, then transfer to an ovenproof dish, cover and cook in the preheated oven for 1 hour. Stir the pork once or twice during cooking. Season with wine vinegar and salt to taste, then serve with thread egg noodles.

SAVOURY MUSHROOM AND BACON MINCE

SERVES 4–5

A family favourite with a mighty tang that is quick to prepare at the end of the working day.

4 rashers streaky bacon,	*8oz (225g) mushrooms,*
rinded and chopped	*sliced*
1 large onion, sliced	*14oz (400g) can cream*
1lb (460g) minced beef	*of mushroom soup*
1tsp Marmite yeast	*freshly ground black*
extract	*pepper*

Cook the bacon and onion together in a non-stick pan until the onion is soft – if no such pan is avail-able add just a little oil to the mixture to prevent it from burning. Add the minced beef with the yeast extract and brown thoroughly. Stir in the mushrooms and continue cooking until they are soft, then add the soup. Bring to the boil, then simmer for 25 minutes.

Season with pepper before serving if necessary.

POST OFFICE PIZZAS

SERVES 4–6

None of the Windsors ever think that there is enough topping on a bought pizza – even one from their own shop! So this is how they quickly prepare pizzas that are acceptable. Make two different pizzas and have a slice of each.

two 10in (25cm)	*9oz (250g) jar pizza*
prepared pizza bases	*topping sauce*

Preheat the oven to 220°C/425°F/Gas mark 7. Place the pizza bases on baking sheets and spread evenly with the sauce, then add the toppings. Bake in the oven for 15 minutes, finishing the egg under the grill if it is not cooked to your liking.

FOR TOPPING 1

6oz (175g) frozen	*2oz (60g) mushrooms*
chopped spinach	*2oz (50g) can anchovy*
freshly ground black	*fillets, chopped*
pepper	*1 egg*

Heat the spinach in a pan until just defrosted then cook until any water has evaporated. Spread it over one of the pizzas, making a well in the centre, then season the spinach with plenty of pepper. Make a ring of the sliced mushrooms and chopped anchovies on top of the spinach then break the egg into the centre. Season again with pepper and pour the oil from the anchovies over the pizza.

FOR TOPPING 2

2oz (60g) Italian	*5oz (150g) mozzarella,*
salami, thinly sliced	*sliced*
1 green pepper, seeded	*olives or capers to taste*
and cut into rings	*1tbsp olive oil*
2oz (60g) mushrooms	

Arrange the salami over the remaining pizza and top with the pepper rings, sliced mushrooms and moz-zarella. Add olives or capers to taste and season with black pepper. Drizzle the olive oil over the cheese.

The interesting thing about Viv's recipes is the fact that they are very economical, and the ingredients are easy to get hold of. Viv makes Scott and Kelly watch as she believes that soon they will be leading their own independent lives; and until that time they can always help in the kitchen.

The Windsor family is only just settling in to Emmerdale. The past couple of years – since coming up north – have been quite turbulent for them all. They're loud and brash, but I think the world of them. Viv's selection of recipes reflects their personalites.

I like the way Viv is open to change and able to adapt to what her children like. The trip to Florida impressed them enormously, and Viv's efforts to recreate American fast food on a budget are highly imaginative, quick and easy to prepare.

TEX-MEX
CHICKEN CASSEROLE

SERVES 5

The Windsors all like Tex-Mex food – they got a taste for it when they went to Disney World.

3tbsp oil	*4oz (120g) frozen peas*
8–10 chicken thighs, skinned	*14oz (400g) can red kidney beans, drained (optional)*
1 packet taco seasoning mix	*salt and freshly ground black pepper*
14oz (400g) can chopped tomatoes	*boiled rice and tortilla chips to serve*
4oz (120g) frozen sweetcorn	

Dredge the chicken in the taco seasoning, then fry in the hot oil in a large frying-pan over a medium heat until the chicken is browned on both sides – do not cook too quickly as the taco seasoning may burn and become bitter. Add the chopped tomatoes and half a can measure of water; rinse the can round to get all the benefit of the tomatoes. Bring the casserole to the boil, then cover and simmer for 45 minutes, until the chicken is tender.

Stir the frozen vegetables and kidney beans, if used, into the pan. Return the mixture to the boil and simmer, uncovered, for 5 minutes, then season to taste before serving with rice and tortilla chips.

HEARTY
BOLOGNESE BAKE

SERVES 4–5

Although this recipe requires more cooking time than a conventional spaghetti bolognese, it appeals to Viv as it can be prepared in advance and then just reheated at the end of a busy working day, to give a filling and tasty family supper. Viv sometimes uses a seasoning mix from the shop for the meat sauce if she is short of time, but she prefers to cook from scratch when pressures allow.

1tbsp oil	*salt and freshly ground black pepper*
1 large onion, finely sliced	*8oz (225g) pasta shapes of your choice*
1 clove garlic, sliced	*3oz (90g) Cheddar cheese, grated*
1lb (460g) minced beef	*1tbsp Parmesan cheese, grated (optional)*
1tsp dried mixed herbs	
1 large carrot, sliced	
14oz (400g) can chopped tomatoes	

Cook the onion in the oil in a large pan until soft, then add the garlic and beef and cook until browned. Stir in the herbs, carrots, tomatoes and seasoning, bring to the boil then simmer, covered, for 20–25 minutes. Meanwhile, cook the pasta in a large pan of boiling salted water for 12 minutes, or as directed on the packet.

Preheat the oven to 200°C/400°F/Gas 6. Mix together the sauce and pasta and transfer to a suitable ovenproof dish. Scatter the cheese over the top, then bake for 20–25 minutes, or 30–40 minutes from cold. The cheese will be browned and bubbling when the bake is ready.

MEDITERRANEAN
CAULIFLOWER CHEESE

SERVES 5

A classic family favourite given a holiday flavour by the simple addition of a can of ratatouille. Viv likes to make her own sauce – use a packet mix if you are in a hurry.

1 large cauliflower, cut into florets	*4oz (120g) Cheddar cheese, grated*
3/4pt (430ml) water	*salt and freshly ground black pepper*
3tbsp dried milk powder	*13oz (375g) can ratatouille*
1 1/2oz (45g) butter	
1 1/2oz (45g) flour	

Preheat the oven to 200°C/400°F/Gas 6. Cook the cauliflower in boiling, salted water for 10 minutes then drain, reserving the water. Place the cauliflower in an ovenproof dish. Measure ³/4pt (430ml) of the water and whisk the powdered milk into it. Pour into a saucepan and add the butter and flour. Bring to the boil, whisking constantly, then stir in half the cheese and season to taste.

Pour the ratatouille over the cauliflower then top the dish with the cheese sauce. Scatter with the remaining cheese then bake in the preheated oven for 20–30 minutes, until browned.

CHOCOLATE TRAY BAKE
with Fudge Topping

CUTS INTO 16 PIECES

Viv doesn't have much time for baking but this recipe is really quick to prepare – it's made with mayonnaise which makes a very moist cake. The fudge topping is made with cream cheese and is deliciously different.

Not surprisingly the Windsor kids enjoy helping Viv with the preparation – and then it's a fight to the death to see who licks out the bowl!

8oz (225g) self-raising flour	*8oz (225g) caster sugar*
¹/2tsp salt	*7fl oz (200ml) mayonnaise*
1tsp baking powder	*8fl oz (225ml) water*
2oz (60g) cocoa powder	*1tsp vanilla essence*

FOR THE FUDGE TOPPING

7oz (200g) plain chocolate	*7oz (200g) tub cream cheese*

Preheat the oven to 180°C/350°F/Gas 4 and line a 8x12in (20x30cm) tin with non-stick baking parchment or greased greaseproof paper.

Sieve the flour, salt, baking powder and cocoa together, then add the sugar and sieve again into a large bowl. Whisk the mayonnaise, water and vanilla essence together, pour into the dry ingredients and whisk together quickly until well blended. Pour into the prepared tin, lightly smooth the top and bake for 35 minutes. Turn onto a wire rack and allow to cool.

Melt the chocolate for the topping in a bowl over a pan of water or in the microwave, whisk then allow to cool slightly. Beat the cream cheese until soft then add the chocolate and beat again. Spread the mixture over the tray bake, then leave until the topping is set. Cut into squares to serve.

BONFIRE NIGHT SUPPER

November nights are traditionally cold and dark, but in Emmerdale the advent of bonfire night for some reason causes temperatures to rise and passions to burn. Guy Fawkes may be the toast of the fifth of November around the nation, but in our little community we remember it for other events.

The fifth of November will remain etched in the mind of Rachel Hughes forever. Bonfire Night was when Pete Whiteley, her married boyfriend, told Rachel that their relationship was over. Nobody knew why Rachel wept as the fire burned and the flames lit up the sky. She'd kept the affair secret, at his request. Later it was to become public knowledge, and fireworks of a more metaphorical nature were to explode in Rachel's face, but that's another story.

Frank Tate organised his first bonfire at Home Farm to celebrate Christopher's marriage to Kathy.

The married couple were flown back by helicopter to witness the brightest fireworks display Emmerdale had ever seen. Kathy and Christopher's names were lit up across the night sky. There are some people who say that Frank Tate has no taste, but I say the man has style.

I introduced Shirley to my Emmerdale friends at an Emmerdale Farm bonfire party. She was apprehensive, but it turned out she had nothing to worry about – she ended up helping in the kitchen, as usual. More recently Frank invited me along to a bonfire supper at Home Farm. It was a relief to find that the only explosive elements around that night were in the fireworks! The evening passed without incident, and we all tucked into homemade toffee apples, cakes and savouries. Mr Fawkes was the only bad guy around that night!

MEXICAN CATHERINE WHEELS

MAKES ABOUT 32

A cold Bonfire Night is quickly warmed by these fiery Catherine Wheels. Add as many chillis as you think your guests can take – the Emmerdale Bonfire Party is held at Home Farm, and Kim and Frank enjoy spicy food! These wheels keep well and may be made a day or two before a party. Leave the bacon out of some if you are expecting some vegetarians, but remember which Catherine Wheels have the no-meat filling!

6 rashers streaky bacon, rinded	1tbsp freshly chopped coriander leaf or 1tsp dried
7oz (200g) cream cheese	3tbsp taco sauce or tomato salsa
1 small onion, finely chopped	salt
1 clove garlic, crushed	4oz (120g) cheese, grated or crumbled
1–2 green chillis, very finely chopped	
3oz (90g) pitted black olives, chopped	
1tsp chilli powder	8 flour tortillas

Grill the bacon until crispy, then chop it into small pieces. Beat the cream cheese until soft, then add the bacon and all the remaining filling ingredients. Spread the mixture evenly over the tortillas, then place one on top of another to give four double stacks. Roll up tightly, like Swiss rolls, and wrap in plastic wrap then chill for 2 hours.

Preheat the oven to 200°C/400°F/Gas 6. Unwrap the tortilla rolls and trim away the ends. Cut each roll into 8 slices about 1/2in (1.25cm) thick. Place on baking sheets, not too close together, and bake for 12–15 minutes, until golden brown. Cool slightly then serve.

LENTIL, ORANGE AND TOMATO SOUP

SERVES 6

This economical soup is ideal for large gatherings – the secret of a really good flavour is not to allow the soup to boil once the orange juice is added or it will become slightly bitter.

2tbsp oil	4oz (120g) orange lentils
1 large onion, finely sliced	1 orange, grated rind and juice
14oz (400g) can chopped tomatoes	salt and freshly ground black pepper
2pt (1.1l) vegetable or chicken stock	2 bay leaves

Cook the onion in the oil until soft in a large saucepan, then add all the remaining ingredients except the orange juice and bring to the boil. Cover and simmer for 30 minutes. Remove the bay leaves and allow the soup to cool slightly. Pour into a liquidiser or food processor and blend until smooth.

Rinse the pan and return the soup to it. Add the orange juice and season to taste, then reheat gently, if necessary, and serve.

Do not boil the soup once the orange juice has been added, as the flavour will spoil.

STARBURST SALAD

SERVES 8–10

Finger food at barbecues and bonfire parties is often chops, drumsticks and other easy-to-eat meats – fine for carnivores but not so good for vegetarians! This pasta salad will satisfy anyone who doesn't eat meat and may be prepared well in advance, but do not add the mayonnaise until about an hour before you serve it, to keep all the ingredients fresh and crisp. Flavour the dressing with garlic if you wish.

17oz (500g) pasta shapes – spirals, twists or small shells	8oz (225g) Edam cheese, diced
2 red peppers, seeded and diced	salt and freshly ground black pepper
2 green peppers, seeded and diced	1–2tbsp freshly chopped mixed herbs
2 large carrots, peeled and diced	1/2pt (280ml) mayonnaise
1 bunch spring onions, finely chopped	1/4pt (150ml) natural yogurt
14oz (400g) can red kidney beans, drained and rinsed	paprika to garnish

Cook the pasta in plenty of boiling, salted water as directed, then drain, rinse and allow to cool.

Place the cold pasta in a serving dish and add all the remaining ingredients except the mayonnaise and yogurt. Blend them together with a little seasoning and add them to the salad about 1 hour before serving, tossing well to make certain that all the pasta, vegetables and beans are coated. Garnish with a little paprika and serve.

Frank Tate reminded me of a strange occurrence one bonfire night several years ago, before he moved into the area. At the time he'd been negotiating to purchase Home Farm. On the night of 5 November he'd returned to the big house for a look around the grounds. Driving back through the village he almost knocked down two idiots who ran across the road in front of him clutching a guy. The two idiots turned out to be Seth Armstrong and Archie Brooks. Frank had never bothered to ask them what they were up to that night, and he wondered if I knew anything about it. I did. You see, Seth and Archie were in charge of the village bonfire that year. Archie made the guy and Seth, who had been charged with the task of finding something for it to wear, just happened to come across an old discarded suit. Unfortunately Seth had found *my* best suit which I had put aside to take to the dry cleaners. I was most annoyed to see it go up in smoke. Frank found it very amusing. 'One day,' Archie said at the time, 'you'll look back on this and laugh' – and do you know, for the first time since it happened, I did!

HALLOWE'EN PUMPKIN SOUP

SERVES 6

There are plenty of pumpkins about in November and anyone who has made a pumpkin lantern for Hallowe'en will welcome a few suggestions for using up the pumpkin flesh. If you have a large pumpkin you can make a vast quantity of soup!

1oz (30g) butter	1lb (460g) prepared
1 large onion, finely	pumpkin flesh, diced
sliced	1¹/2pt (850ml) vegetable
1 clove garlic, crushed	stock
(optional)	salt and black pepper
1 tsp ground coriander	1pt (570ml) milk
12oz (340g) swede or	freshly chopped
parsnip, peeled and	coriander to garnish
diced	(optional)

Melt the butter in a large pan, then add the onion, garlic and ground coriander and cook slowly until the onion is soft. Stir in the swede or parsnip, and the pumpkin, then add the stock with a little salt and pepper. Bring the soup to the boil, then cover and simmer for 30 minutes. Allow the soup to cool slight-

ly then pour into a liquidiser or food processor and blend until smooth. Add the milk, season to taste and reheat until almost boiling. Serve garnished with chopped coriander if you wish.

GUY FAWKES' BAKED BANANAS
with Lemon Butter

SERVES 4

Baked bananas are the easiest of desserts to prepare for an outdoor event like a bonfire party. Their only drawback is that they can be too sickly and sweet but the tang of the lemon butter in this recipe gives them a delicious flavour. Serve with a scoop of vanilla ice cream if you are not catering for too many people at your party.

1 lemon, grated rind	sugar to taste
and juice	4 small bananas
1¹/2oz (40g) unsalted	
butter	

Beat the lemon rind, juice and butter together and sweeten with sugar if necessary. You may not need all the juice from the lemon. Leave until required.

Preheat the oven to 200°C/400°F/Gas 6 if cooking the bananas indoors – they are also suitable for cooking in the embers of a bonfire or on a barbecue. Prick the bananas lightly with a fork then wrap them tightly in foil, making certain that the parcels will be easy to unwrap when cooked and hot. Bake for about 15-20 minutes. Partially unwrap the bananas and slit them open lengthways, cutting into the fruits. Place a knob of the butter on each banana and allow it to melt before eating from the foil package with a teaspoon. Serve the bananas in bowls if you intend to offer ice cream with them.

SATAY CHICKEN DRUMSTICKS

SERVES 4

Kim Tate brings a touch of the Orient to Emmerdale's bonfire party.

8 skinless chicken drumsticks

FOR THE MARINADE

2tbsp natural yogurt	1 lemon, rind and juice
1tbsp oil (chilli oil works	2tbsp satay marinade
really well)	sauce

Mix together all the ingredients for the marinade. Make two deep slashes in each of the drumsticks then add them to the marinade, turning them over to ensure that they are well coated. Leave for 2–3 hours.

Preheat the oven to 220°C/425°F/Gas 7. Place the drumsticks on a wire rack over a roasting tin and cook in the oven for about 30–40 minutes, basting once or twice with any remaining marinade. Serve hot or cold.

RIKRAK RIBS

SERVES 6

Why is it that any food that you eat in your fingers outside tastes so good? Line the baking tin with foil before cooking these ribs – it will make the washing up an awful lot easier.

2tbsp clear honey	1tsp Dijon mustard
2tbsp hoi-sin sauce	6 pork spare ribs

Preheat the oven to 200°C/400°F/Gas 6. Mix together the honey, hoi-sin sauce and mustard. Place the ribs in a small, foil-lined roasting tin and pour the sauce over. Roast in the preheated oven for 40–50 minutes, depending on size, turning once.

LIGHTNING TOFFEE

MAKES ABOUT 1LB (460G)

There's something very northern about treacle toffee – dark, buttery and delicious. The most important thing is to cut it into small pieces, otherwise the carollers may not be ready to start singing the next song!

1lb (460g) demerara	4oz (120g) black treacle
sugar	3oz (90g) unsalted
1/4pt (150ml) water	butter
4oz (120g) golden syrup	1/2tsp cream of tartar

Butter a 7in (17.5cm) square or similar tin. Dissolve the sugar in the water in a large, heavy-based saucepan. Add the remaining ingredients and stir until the butter is dissolved. Bring to the boil then boil slowly for about 15 minutes, stirring from time to time, until the mixture reaches soft crack stage (132°C/270°F). Pour the toffee immediately into the prepared tin, then leave to cool before marking into squares. Break or cut the toffee into pieces when completely cold and set.

PINK COCONUT ICE

MAKES JUST OVER 1LB (460G)

Coconut Ice is fairly economical and is a good thing for children to make (with a little adult supervision at the critical moments!). If you want to make pink-and-white coconut ice, warm a bowl with hot water whilst the sugar syrup is boiling, then throw away the water and use the bowl to colour the first lot of coconut ice. Leave the remaining mixture in the pan until required, as this will keep it soft and workable.

1lb (460g) granulated	5oz (150g) desiccated
sugar	coconut
1/4pt (150ml) milk	red food colouring

Butter a tin about 6x8in (15x20cm). Dissolve the sugar slowly in the milk in a large saucepan, stirring from time to time. Bring to the boil, then boil slowly for about 10 mins, until the mixture reaches soft ball stage (116°C/240°F).

Remove the pan from the heat and quickly beat in the coconut. Pour half the mixture into the tin, colour the remainder with a few drops of colouring, then pour it quickly in an even layer over the white layer in the tin. Leave to cool then mark into squares. Cut when completely cold. Store in a sweet tin or jar.

ALAN TURNER ENTERTAINS

It wouldn't take me long to choose my perfect dinner-date partner; it would be my dear friend Caroline Bates. This wonderful woman came to work as my secretary when I was Estate Manager at Home Farm. She very quickly put my office in order, and then my life. I think that was when I fell in love with her. It was several years before I was brave enough to pluck up the courage to tell her how I felt, but I proposed to her and she accepted. I can't say it all ended happily ever after. Before we were due to step down the aisle together Caroline's mother moved in with us…and that was when it all went wrong. Caroline cancelled the wedding and moved away to Scarborough to look after the old dear! After that our meetings were fleeting and painful. I pro-

posed to her again much later on, but it was not to be. I loved Shirley, my wife, with all my heart and I miss her terribly…yet still I feel drawn to Caroline. I don't have the heart to invite her to dinner as anything but a friend. I could never propose to her again for fear of being at best rebuked, at worst ridiculed. The recipes I have chosen are favourites of Caroline's and I hope you enjoy them. For me they bring back memories of coy dinners for two, of her sparkling eyes and softly whispered conversations.

This meal is chosen for its strong and exciting flavours. It is primarily a summer meal, although it would also cheer a long winter's evening. I serve a mixed salad with the main course but no rice or potatoes – they really are not needed.

ITALIAN-STYLE FRIED COURGETTE SALAD

SERVES 2

Theme an Italian supper and the most obvious starter is mixed anti-pasto, a selection of cold meats and salads, which is sublimely delicious. Serve this salad with a small selection of salami, or just with Italian bread.

1 small onion, preferably red, finely sliced	1tsp white wine vinegar
3tbsp fruity olive oil	salt and freshly ground black pepper
2 small courgettes, trimmed and sliced	1tbsp pine kernels
	3–4 fresh basil leaves, torn into small pieces

Cook the onion slowly in the olive oil for about 5 minutes until soft but not browned. Remove to a dish using a slotted spoon so that the oil stays in the pan. Add the courgettes (sliced diagonally) and fry quickly for 4–5 minutes, until browned on both sides, then add to the onions and stir.

Add the vinegar to the oil in the pan with a little salt and pepper, stir briefly over the heat then pour the dressing over the vegetables. Add the pine kernels to the pan and cook for 1–2 minutes. Leave the courgettes until cool, then stir in the basil and toasted pine kernels and transfer to a serving dish. Serve at room temperature for maximum flavour.

MEDITERRANEAN CHICKEN
with Sun Dried Tomato Sauce

SERVES 2

This dish positively zings with flavour! It can turn the dullest Emmerdale evening into a sunny occasion.

FOR THE MARINADE	2 part-boned chicken breasts, skinned
4tbsp fruity olive oil	1 small onion, finely chopped
1tbsp sherry vinegar	6 halves sun dried tomatoes, finely shredded
1 lemon, grated rind and juice	1/4pt (150ml) single cream
salt and freshly ground black pepper	6 fresh basil leaves, torn
3–4 leaves fresh basil, torn	salt and freshly ground black pepper

Mix together all the ingredients for the marinade, add the chicken breasts and spoon some of the marinade over them. Leave for at least 2 hours.

Preheat the oven to 200°C/400°F/Gas 6. Drain the chicken breasts then roast them for 45 minutes, basting from time to time.

Cook the onion in any remaining marinade in a pan until soft then add the shredded tomatoes and cook for a further 2–3 minutes. Add the cream and basil leaves then blend until smooth in a liquidiser or food processor. Season to taste then serve the sauce spooned over the chicken.

BROCCOLI WITH GORGONZOLA

SERVES 2

I'd like to have this on The Woolpack menu, but I am not sure that Emmerdale is quite ready for it!

2 large heads broccoli, trimmed and cut into florets	1½oz (45g) walnut pieces, roughly chopped
2oz (60g) Gorgonzola cheese, crumbled with a fork	freshly ground black pepper

Cook the broccoli in boiling salted water until just tender, then drain and place in an ovenproof serving dish. Mix the cheese and walnuts together and scatter them over the broccoli then cook under a preheated grill until the cheese has just melted. Season with plenty of black pepper and serve.

FRESH MANGO WITH PASSION FRUIT AND LEMON

SERVES 2

Only a light dessert is required after this meal, but it has to be one with plenty of flavour or it will be lost. This combination of exotic fruits and lemon is ideal.

1 large ripe mango	1 lime
2 passion fruits, as wrinkled as possible	1tbsp caster sugar, or to taste

Pass a knife through the middle of the mango and let it follow the stone to remove the flesh. Score through the flesh to the skin, cutting the fruit into cubes, do not cut through the skin. Press up gently on the skin, turning the fruit inside-out to form a hedgehog, then place each one on an individual serving plate.

Squeeze the juice from the lime and mix it with the seeds from the passion fruits – scoop these out of the half shells using a teaspoon. Add the sugar to taste, then spoon the mixture over the mango, or onto the plate to one side of the fruit.

The recipes in this section are good and trusty favourites of mine, and have been well received on many occasions. I once met a woman called Rosemary who was prepared to marry me on the strength of my Mussel and Saffron Soup alone! Actually, she was quite mad; luckily, dinner for two with Rosemary turned out to be a one-off event.

Don't be fooled by these recipes. They look, and are, quite simple, but the overall effects in terms of taste and aroma is one of sophistication, an important quality when trying to impress. As for the wine, two or three years ago I would have stuck strictly to the traditional rule of red wine for dark meat and white wine for fish and poultry. Shirley, my dear departed wife, was of the opinion that it didn't matter what colour wine you drank as long as it was of decent quality and you appreciated it. I tend to go along with that. It should also be drunk in the company of good friends.

This is a more traditional meal but it is nevertheless special in the choice and combination of ingredients and in the care required for their cooking.

MUSSEL AND SAFFRON SOUP

SERVES 2

I love mussels but it is not always easy to get them in the shell, even from the suppliers for The Woolpack. This soup is that it can be made with frozen or canned mussels, although fresh are best.

1oz (30g) butter	*1 bay leaf*
1 small onion, finely chopped	*1 sachet powdered saffron*
2 sticks celery, finely chopped	*8oz (225g) canned or frozen mussels*
1 small clove garlic, crushed	*salt and freshly ground black pepper*
³/4pt (430ml) good fish stock	*1tbsp freshly chopped parsley*

Melt the butter in a pan, add the onion, celery and garlic and cook slowly until soft, then add the stock, bay leaf and saffron and bring slowly to the boil. Simmer the soup for 15 minutes then allow it to cool slightly before blending in a liquidiser or food processor until smooth.

Return to the pan and add the mussels. Heat gently for 5 minutes, until the mussels are piping hot, season to taste and garnish with the parsley.

GAMMON STEAKS WITH WHITBY CHEESE

SERVES 2

I enjoyed this dish in a pub up on the moors on a rare day off. Sadly I forgot to ask the landlord for its history, but determined to recreate the flavours of onions, cheese and cream on my return. The sauce is quickly prepared while the gammon is grilling.

2 gammon steaks, about 4–6oz (125–175g) each	*3¹/2oz (100g) cream cheese*
1tbsp olive oil	*salt and freshly ground black pepper*
1 small onion, very finely chopped	*freshly chopped chives to garnish*
4–5tbsp double cream	

Grill the gammon steaks for 5 minutes on each side until cooked, or as directed. Meanwhile, cook the onion in the oil until soft but not browned. Add the double cream and the cream cheese and heat gently until the cheese has melted and the sauce is thick. Season to taste then serve the sauce poured over the gammon. Garnish with freshly chopped chives.

MANGETOUT
with Shredded Carrots in Orange Juice

SERVES 2

Gammon Steaks with Whitby Cheese requires colourful vegetables with a light flavour to accompany it. This is a delightful way of serving mangetout, which make a perfect accompaniment to gammon.

1 medium carrot, cut into fine matchsticks	*6oz (175g) mangetout, topped and tailed*
juice of 1 large orange, or 3–4fl oz (90–120ml) orange juice	*salt and freshly ground black pepper*

Cut the carrot sticks into 2in (5cm) lengths, then put them in a pan with the orange juice and bring to the boil. Add the mangetout, then cover the pan and steam the vegetables for 4–6 minutes, until the mangetout are just cooked and still bright green in colour. Season with salt and pepper, then serve.

MARMALADE PEAR TARTS

SERVES 2

This is my own recipe, combining one of my favourite fruits with the tangy flavour of orange marmalade in a crumbly pastry case. I use the same pastry as for The Woolpack Christmas mince pies, but one quantity is more than enough for two tarts so I freeze the remainder for later use.

1 quantity orange pastry (see page 21)	*2fl oz (60ml) white wine*
2 small Conference pears, peeled, cored and halved	*2tbsp orange marmalade*
	¹/4pt (150ml) water

Preheat the oven to 190°C/375°F/Gas 5. Roll out a little of the pastry to line two 4in (10cm) flan tins, prick the bases and bake blind (lined with baking parchment and filled with baking beans) for 15 minutes. Remove the beans and paper and cook for a further 5–10 minutes, until browned.

Poach the pears while the pastry is cooking. Bring the wine, marmalade and water to the boil in a small frying-pan, then reduce the heat until the liquid is just simmering. Add the prepared pear halves and simmer for about 10 minutes, until just soft – turn the pears over in the pan as necessary.

Cut the pears so that you can fan them and place two halves in each pastry shell. Return the poaching liquid to the heat and cook until thickened, then pour the syrup evenly over the pears.

Preheat the grill and quickly heat the tarts until the syrup caramelises on the fruit – push any marmalade peel down the sides of the pears so that it does not burn. Serve the tarts warm.

SUMMER FRUITS PUDDING

MAKES 2 INDIVIDUAL PUDDINGS

Summer pudding is one of my favourite desserts (and I tend to make it even when the fruits are out of season – the frozen mixed berries available in supermarkets work just as well as the fresh fruits). I make the puddings in individual moulds left from the wine bar but tea cups work just as well. Always use freshly-cut bread for this pudding – commercially sliced bread has quite the wrong texture and becomes very soggy.

12oz (340g) prepared summer fruits	*whipped cream for serving*
1¹/2oz (45g) granulated sugar	*two small stalks of redcurrants for decoration (optional)*
6–8 slices freshly cut white bread from a small loaf	

Stew the fruits together in a pan for about 5 minutes, until they have produced lots of juice but the berries still retain their shape. Allow to cool.

Trim the crusts from the bread and use to line two individual moulds or tea cups – pack the pieces tightly to form a lining with no gaps. Remove the pieces carefully, one by one, and dip them in the juices from the fruits before placing them in the basin – this ensures that the bread will all be coloured by the fruit juice and that the finished puddings will not be patchy in colour!

Turn the fruits into the lined moulds then cover the tops with bread which has been turned in the juice to colour it too. Place saucers over the moulds and weight them lightly. Chill the puddings for 3–4 hours or overnight.

DINGLE DELIGHTS

I was sitting in the back room of The Woolpack one evening, with a glass of wine, congratulating myself on the near completion of my recipe book, when I was disturbed by a most frightful din at the door. I thought someone was trying to break in. I rushed to open it – Nellie Dingle stood on the threshold, a horrible expression on her fearsome face. I knew I was in for trouble…and I was. She'd discovered that the Dingles were the only family I hadn't approached for recipe contributions. I told her, politely of course, that I wasn't aware she could cook – after all, this was the woman who complained to me that The Woolpack soup of the day tasted different every time she had it! I had visions of her standing over a large, bubbling cauldron in the middle of the woods, throwing in any poor, unfortunate creature that happened to be within shooting distance of the pot.

As it turned out, I was wrong. Nellie has kept her large family healthy and well fed – she gave me some very pleasant, if simple, recipes which I've included here. She told me that at school she came top of the class in cookery – on the day she decided to attend! Obviously it was a day well spent.

NELLIE'S SAUSAGE TOAD
with Thick Onion Gravy

SERVES 6

Zak's favourite meal is sausage and chips and, to make the sausages go further when feeding her hungry men, Nellie usually cooks them in batter as a Toad in the Hole. Zak loves gravy with his Sausage Toad, and Sam's favourite meal is onion gravy with liver and baked beans. Even I am forced to admit that Nellie is onto a good idea with this gravy, and I've developed my own version with flour and gravy browning, garlic, a little red wine and a tablespoon or so of freshly chopped sage.

FOR THE SAUSAGE TOAD

2lbs (900g) thick pork sausages	*8oz (225g) plain flour pinch of salt*
1oz (30g) lard, or 2 tbsp oil	*1pt (570ml) milk or milk and water mixed*
2 eggs, size 3, beaten	

FOR THE GRAVY

2 tbsps oil	*1pt (570ml) vegetable water*
2 large onions, finely sliced	*salt and freshly ground black pepper to taste*
1 tbsp gravy powder	

To make the sausage toad. Preheat the oven to 220°C/425°F/Gas 7. Prick the sausages thoroughly and place them in a large roasting tin (Nellie uses the one that came with her oven) with the additional fat. Cook the sausages for 15 minutes.

Prepare the batter whilst the sausages are cooking. Whisk together the eggs, flour and salt, then gradually whisk in the milk. Pour the batter over the sausages into the hot fat in the tin and cook for a further 45 minutes, until the batter is browned and crisp. Serve with chips and thick onion gravy.

To make the onion gravy. Cook the onions in the oil over a medium-high heat until they are softened and well browned. It is important to brown the onions to add a rich colour and flavour to the gravy.

Stir in the gravy powder and cook gently for a few seconds. Gradually add the vegetable water, stirring

all the time to prevent lumps from forming. Stir the gravy over a medium heat until it boils, then simmer for 1–2 minutes. Season to taste before serving.

SPAGHETTI WITH MEATBALLS

SERVES 4–5

Spaghetti is Nellie's favourite dish, although she generally doesn't like foreign food. As Butch won't eat anything green Nellie has had to devise her own sauces to serve with spaghetti, and her favourite is with meatballs. When time is short she has been known to heat up faggots in onion gravy to serve with pasta, but this is how she makes the dish when she has time.

1lb (460g) minced beef	*1tsp dried mixed herbs*
salt and freshly ground	*1 egg, size 3, beaten*
black pepper	*two 14oz (400g) cans*
2tbsp tomato purée	*chopped tomatoes*
4oz (120g) fat bacon,	*12oz (340g) spaghetti,*
minced	*freshly cooked*
4oz (120g) fresh white	*grated cheese for serving,*
breadcrumbs	*either Cheddar or*
1 onion, minced	*Parmesan*

Place the minced beef in a large bowl, season with salt and pepper and mix in the tomato purée with a wooden spoon. Add the bacon, breadcrumbs, onions and herbs then bind the mixture together with the beaten egg. Shape into walnut-sized meatballs – the mixture should make about 30.

Fry the meatballs until browned on all sides, turning them carefully so that they do not break up – it should not be necessary to add any fat to the frying-pan while cooking the meatballs. Add the chopped tomatoes and as much water or stock as necessary to cover, then bring to the boil and simmer slowly for 20–25 minutes.

Meanwhile cook the spaghetti in plenty of boiling, salted water for 12 minutes, or as directed on the packet. Drain and serve on individual plates, topped with the meatballs, sauce and grated cheese.

JAM AND APPLE SPONGE PUDDING

SERVES 6

The Dingle men have always got room for a pudding. This sponge pudding is quick and filling – any leftovers are just as good cold! Serve with custard, cream or ice cream.

2–3tbsp apricot jam	*2 eggs, size 3, beaten*
12oz (340g) cooking	*4oz (120g) self-raising*
apples, peeled, cored	*flour*
and sliced	*pinch of salt*
4oz (120g) block	*pinch of ground*
margarine	*cinnamon*
4oz (120g) caster sugar	

Preheat the oven to 190°C/375°F/Gas 5. Lightly grease a 8in (20cm) ovenproof flan dish and line the bottom with silicone paper. Spread the jam over the paper and top with the sliced apples.

Cream the margarine and sugar together until pale and fluffy then beat in the eggs, one at a time. Mix together the flour, salt and cinnamon and fold them into the mixture. Spoon the sponge mixture over the apples, spreading it evenly. Bake in the preheated oven for 25–30 minutes, until the sponge is golden brown and springs back when pressed lightly.

Leave the sponge to cool for 2–3 minutes before turning out onto a serving plate. Serve sliced – the Dingles like thick custard with their pudding.

RECIPE INDEX

The Old Mill (Mill Cottage)

The Malt Shovel

The Allotments

Bowling Green

Village Hall

1 Pollard's Cottage
2 Seth and Betty
3 Windsor's Post Office
4 McAllister's Surgery   (The Old Hall)

The Woolpack

1
2
3

Church Yard

St. Mary'
Church

Veterinary Surgery

Geoff Thomas' Farm

4

The Old Schoo
Tearoom

Demdyke Row